THE
FLORA

THE
FLORA

AN ANTHOLOGY OF
POETRY AND PROSE

Compiled by
Fiona MacMath

ILLUSTRATED BY
LIL TUDOR-CRAIG

A LION BOOK

Oxford · Batavia · Sydney

Compilation copyright © 1990 Fiona MacMath
This edition copyright © Lion Publishing
Illustration copyright © Lil Tudor-Craig

Published by
Lion Publishing plc
Sandy Lane West, Oxford, England
ISBN 0 7459 1840 9
Lion Publishing Corporation
1705 Hubbard Avenue, Batavia, Illinois 60510, USA
ISBN 0 7459 1840 9
Albatross Books Pty Ltd
PO Box 320, Sutherland, NSW 2232, Australia
ISBN 0 7324 0191 7

First edition 1990

British Library Cataloguing in Publication Data
The flora: poetry and prose on God, nature and humankind.
 1. Literature. Special subjects. Plants. Anthologies
 I. MacMath, Fiona
 808.8036

 ISBN 0-7459-1840-9

Library of Congress Cataloging-in-Publication Data
The Flora: poetry and prose on God, nature, and humankind / compiled
 by Fiona MacMath. — 1st ed.
 ISBN 0-7459-1840-9
 1. God—Literary collections. 2. Nature—Literary collections.
 3. Man—Literary collections. I. MacMath, Fiona.
 PN6071.G57F58 1990
 808.8'035—dc20

Printed and bound in Great Britain

ACKNOWLEDGMENTS

The following poems or prose extracts are copyright, and I am grateful to the publishers listed for their permission to include their material.

'To Grimwold, Abbot of St Gall' by Strabo (tr. Helen Waddell) from *Medieval Latin Lyrics*, reprinted by permission of Constable Publishers.

'The Punishment' by Laurence Lerner, from *Chapter and Verse*, reprinted by permission of Martin Secker and Warburg Limited.

'The Burning of the Leaves' by Laurence Binyon from *Collected Poems*, reprinted by permission of the Literary Trustees of Laurence Binyon, and the Society of Authors as their representative.

'The Scarecrow' by Walter de la Mare, reprinted by permission of the Literary Trustees of Walter de la Mare, and the Society of Authors as their representative.

Lines from 'The Everlasting Mercy' by John Masefield, reprinted by permission of the Literary Trustees of John Masefield, and the Society of Authors as their representative.

'Morning Glory' and 'Thanksgiving for a Fair Summer' by Ruth Pitter, from *Collected Poems 1926–1966*, published by the Cresset Press, reprinted by permission of Barrie and Jenkins.

'How Many Heavens' by Edith Sitwell, from *Collected Poems*, published by Macmillan, and reprinted by permission of David Higham Associates Limited.

'There is no rose of such vertu' by kind permission of the Master and Fellows of Trinity College, Cambridge.

An extract from *Henrietta's House* by Elizabeth Goudge, published by Hodder and Stoughton, and reprinted by permission of David Higham Associates Limited.

'The Pear Tree' by Clare Girling, from *100 Contemporary Christian Poets* published by Lion Publishing, and reprinted with their permission.

'Olive Trees' by Margaret Orford, from *100 Contemporary Christian Poets* published by Lion Publishing, and reprinted with their permission.

'Immanence' by Evelyn Underhill, reprinted by permission of Tessa Sayle Literary and Dramatic Agency.

'Now the Green Blade Riseth' by J.M.C. Crum, 'Crown of Roses', (tr. G. Dearmer), and 'Es ist ein Ros', (tr. Ursula Vaughan Williams), from *The Oxford Book of Carols*, reprinted by permission of the Oxford University Press.

Extracts from the Authorized (King James) Version of the Bible, the rights of which are vested in the Crown in perpetuity within the United Kingdom, are reproduced by permission of Eyre and Spottiswoode Publishers, Her Majesty's Printers, London.

Extract from *The Book of Beasts* (tr. T.H. White), reprinted by permission of David Higham Associates Limited.

'Vegetation' and 'Seed' by Kathleen Raine, reprinted by permission of the author.

Extract from *Elizabeth and her German Garden* by Elizabeth Von Arnim, reprinted by permission of Virago.

Strenuous efforts have been made by the author to trace the copyright holders of all the material used. If there are any omissions, please let us know so that acknowledgment may be made in future editions.

Special thanks to Paul Handley for his great kindness and skill in translating 'The Dream of the Rood'.

CONTENTS

INTRODUCTION

THE GARDEN

PARADISE

GARDENS FAR IN SPACE AND TIME

LORD JESUS HATH A GARDEN

A CHAPTER OF SAINTS

THE FLOWER GARDEN

A NOSEGAY

THE ROSE GARDEN

THE HOT HOUSE

IN THE ORCHARD

TO THE FIELDS

IN THE WOODS

ELEANOR ROSE

Little girl – here are apples and sweetest
Roses for you; primroses and peaches,
Codlins-and-cream and Lady's Smocks, the scents
Of strawberries and haycocks, for incense;
A daisy chain encircling your head.

Little queen, solemn-faced beneath the daisies,
Your royal progress has begun – small, sweet
Scarlet boots tread their uncertain measure
Over diamond-degged grass. Baby plump hands
Lift pebbles in amazement – royal treasure!

May you walk in this walled garden too,
And turn the leaves, pluck fruit from laden trees.
May you sometimes meet the Gardener and hear
His greeting to you, down-to-earth and clear –
And may you, in your wanderings, snatch a glance
Of Paradise, catch up your skirts and dance.

INTRODUCTION

COME INTO THE GARDEN

Anthologists are without much honour in a gathering of writers – and rightly so. There are times when their work seems to be little more creative than a copy-typist's. They are parasites upon the lovely things of other people: the title of one famous anthology – *Other Men's Flowers* – sums it up well.

Yet perhaps we can claim the sort of creativity that the flower arranger shows. The nice lady who does the flowers in church and the Japanese lady skilled in the art of ikebana do not create the flowers they use, but with them they create their own combination of colour, shape and scent. Both will say that the flowers are not dead material to be twisted and manipulated into a preconceived shape; the best arrangers will be constantly aware of the flowers' own forms and qualities.

This anthology of 'other men's flowers' attempts to celebrate, in prose and verse, the glory of God's creation of flowers, fruits and trees of all kinds, and his very presence in them. Poets down the ages have peered at daisies and seen glimmerings of the eternal. Horticulturalists and herbalists once delighted to draw spiritual lessons from their subjects. Moralists of the eighteenth and nineteenth centuries pointed to the ever-growing world of fruit and flowers opened up by foreign travel. Most pious Victorian and Edwardian ladies were amateur botanists and versifiers; a little of their work is still fresh today. Writers have always sung the praises of their precious gardens. The Bible teems with imagery from plants, seeds, fruits and trees; the world is God's walled garden, his vineyard. Jesus, himself, when he spoke of the kingdom of heaven, spoke of vines, mustard seeds, fig trees, lilies.

And why not? We know already that every green thing on the earth is a vital part of our own life-support system. From plants we must get the food we eat and the air we breathe. We are realizing that we cannot destroy the green things of this planet without destroying ourselves as well. Despite this knowledge, tropical rainforests are razed daily, with nothing but short-term profit and long-term desertification in view. We, who are so much wealthier, are *still* vandalizing the countryside with fertilizers and pesticides, felling trees and pulling up hedgerows in the name of greater short-term productivity.

'Photosynthesis', however, is not the first word that springs to mind when we see the first, palest green shoots in the spring. We love plants for themselves too; their beauty never fails to inspire poets and artists and flower arrangers. And we have 'friends' – a few house plants, a special rose, a tree planted to commemorate a birth or a wedding or someone's life. I write this some time after a hurricane ravaged the southern half of Britain and uprooted fifteen million trees. People mourned those trees, often to their own surprise. They were part of our landscape, and a landscape is both material and spiritual.

I learned to love flowers and trees late on; it's the old story of not appreciating a thing until you have to do without it. After living for two years in a house which boasted a Gertrude Jekyll garden (which I don't think I ever noticed) I spent eight long years in London, five of which were on one of its busiest roads. The gallant geraniums in the window-boxes were furred with exhaust fumes in a few days, and the only thing which flourished at the front of the house was a monstrous weed which was cherished although it threatened the foundations.

But in the back yard we had an elder tree. This was a solace, a screen, a friend, a shelter for an exceptionally clumsy pigeon, a promise of better things to come. It was vastly over-grown and a young aboriculturist said we should cut it down before it fell down. He gave it eighteen months at the very most. We couldn't find it in our hearts to cut that tree down. It was a strange irony of fate that the young man died a few months later. The tree still flourishes.

Then we moved to the country – what a joy it is to live in a place where there is may blossom in May-time and wild roses studding every hedge in June! Some farmers have understood the gospel: there are more wild flowers about now than when I previously lived in the countryside. The only sadness was that so much of the country is inaccessible nowadays, and much of it would not attract walkers and poets even if it were. Even so, it was a wrench to move back to London, though a garden of our own and surrounding trees still provide us with parables and a promise of a return to the countryside one day.

There is a charming children's story about a little girl who is told that when she grows up she can do anything, anything at all, as long as she finds a way to do one thing to make the world a happier place. She grows up to be a teacher and a traveller, and she eventually falls ill. The thing that really makes her well again is the sight of a few lupins growing outside her window – and that gives her the idea of what she could do to carry out her life's task. When she recovers, she spends the rest of her life wandering all over the world, sowing lupin seeds as she goes until, as an old lady, she eventually comes back to her own house and her own tiny garden of lupins.

THE GARDEN

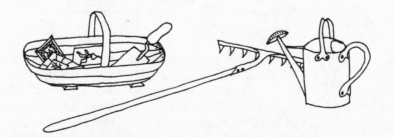

Juniper

Cypress

Mezereon

Anemone

Daffodil

Lilac

God Almighty first planted a garden. And, indeed, it is the purest of human pleasures. It is the greatest refreshment to the spirits of man, without which building and palaces are but gross handyworks: and a man shall ever see, that when ages grow to civility and elegancy, men come to build stately, sooner than to garden finely; as if gardening were the greater perfection.

I do hold it, in the royal ordering of gardens, there ought to be gardens for all the months in the year, in which, severally, things of beauty may be then in season.

For December and January, and the latter part of November, you must take such things as are green all winter; holly, ivy, bays, juniper, cypress-trees, yew, pines, fir-trees, rosemary, lavender; periwinkle, the white, the purple, and the blue; germander, flag, orange-trees, lemon-trees, and myrtles, if they be stoved; and sweet marjoram, warm set.

There followth, for the latter part of January and February, the mezerion-tree, which then blossoms; crocus vernus, both the yellow and the grey; primroses, anemones, the early tulip, hyacinthus orientalis, chamaïris, frettellaria.

For March, there come violets, especially the single blue, which are the earliest; the early daffodil, the daisy, the almond-tree in blossom, the peach-tree in blossom, the cornelian-tree in blossom, sweetbriar.

In April, follow the double white violet, the wall-flower, the stock-gilliflower, the cowslip, flower-de-luces, and lilies of all natures, rosemary flowers, the tulip, the double peony, the pale daffodil, the French honeysuckle, the cherry-tree in blossom, the damascene, and plum-trees in blossom, the white thorn in leaf, the lilac-tree.

In May and June come pinks of all sorts,
especially the blush pink; roses of all kinds, except
the musk, which comes later; honeysuckles,
strawberries, bugloss, columbine, the French
marigold, flos Africanus, cherry-tree in fruit,
ribes, figs in fruit, rasps, vine flowers, lavender in
flowers, the sweet satyrian, with the white flower,
herba muscaria, lilium convallium, the apple-tree
in blossom.

In July come gilliflowers of all varieties, musk
roses, the lime-tree in blossom, early pears, and
plums in fruit, ginnitings, quadlins.

In August come plums of all sorts in fruit, pears,
apricocks, barberries, filberds, musk melons,
monks-hoods of all colours.

In September come grapes, apples, poppies of
all colours, peaches, melocotones, nectarines,
cornelians, wardens, quinces.

In October and the beginning of November come
services, medlars, bullaces, roses cut or removed
to come late, hollyoaks, and such like. These
particulars are for the climate of London; but
my meaning is perceived, that you may have *ver
perpetuum*, as the place affords.

FRANCIS BACON (1561–1626)

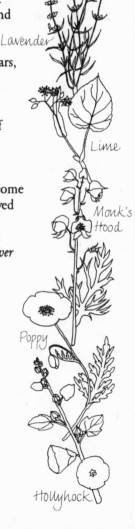

Viper's Bugloss

Lavender

Lime

Monk's Hood

Poppy

Hollyhock

18

For if delight may provoke men's labour, what greater delight is there than to behold the earth apparelled with plants, as with a robe of embroidered work, set with Orient pearls and garnished with great diversity of rare and costly jewels? If this variety and perfection of colours may affect the eye, it is such in herbs and flowers that no Apelles, no Zeuxis, ever could by any art express the like: if odours or if taste may work satisfaction they are both so sovereign in plants and so comfortable that no confection of the apothecaries can equal their excellent virtue. But these delights are in the outward senses; the principal delight is in the mind, singularly enriched with the knowledge of these visible things, setting forth to us the invisible wisdom and admirable workmanship of Almighty God.

JOHN GERARD (1545–1612)
Herbal

IMMANENCE

I come in the little things,
Saith the Lord:
Not borne on morning wings
Of majesty, but I have set My Feet
Amidst the delicate and bladed wheat
That springs triumphant in the furrowed sod.
There so I dwell, in weakness and in power;
Not broken or divided, saith our God!
In your strait garden plot I come to flower:
About your porch My Vine
Meek, fruitful, doth entwine;
Waits, at the threshold, Love's appointed hour . . .

EVELYN UNDERHILL (1875–1941)

20

Feb. 24 In the snow flat-topped hillocks and shoulders outlined with wavy edges, ridge below ridge, very like the grain of wood in line and in projection like relief maps. These the wind makes I think and of course drifts, which are in fact snow waves. The sharp nape of a drift is sometimes broken by slant flutes or channels. I think this must be when the wind after shaping the drift has changed and cast waves in the body of the wave itself. All the world is full of inscape and chance left free to act falls into an order as well as purpose: looking out of my window I caught it in the random clods and broken heaps of snow made by the cast of a broom. The same of the path trenched by footsteps in ankledeep snow across the fields leading to Hodder wood through which we went to see the river. The sun was bright, the broken brambles and all boughs and banks limed and cloyed with white, the brook down the clough pulling its way by drops and by bubbles in turn under a shell of ice.

In **March** there was much snow.

April 8 The ashtree growing in the corner of the garden was felled. It was lopped first: I heard the sound and looking out and seeing it maimed there came at that moment a great pang and I wished to die and not to see the inscapes of the world destroyed any more.

GERARD MANLEY HOPKINS (1844–1889)
From his diary

'TIS WINTER NOW

'Tis winter now; the fallen snow
    Has left the heavens all coldly clear;
Through leafless boughs the sharp winds blow,
    And all the earth lies dead and drear.

And yet God's love is not withdrawn;
    His life within the keen air breathes;
His beauty paints the crimson dawn,
    And clothes the boughs with glittering wreaths.

And though abroad the sharp winds blow,
    And skies are chill, and frosts are keen,
Home closer draws her circle now,
    And warmer glows her light within.

O God! who giv'st the winter's cold,
    As well as summer's joyous rays,
Us warmly in thy love enfold,
    And keep us through life's wintry days.

SAMUEL LONGFELLOW (1819–1892)

22

God of bright colours, rainbows, peacocks,
And the shot-silk gleam of springing
Wind-shaken wheat
On rolling red-ribbed Earth:
Thou Who dost bring to birth
From out the womb
Of darkness golden flowers,
Filling the hollows
With daffodils in March,
Cowslips in April,
Dog-roses in May;
Who in the smouldering forest
Makes the huge
Red flare of Autumn:
God of all the colours
On Earth, and hues (too bright for mortal eyes)
In Paradise –
Unblind me to Thy glory,
That I may see!

F.W. HARVEY (b. 1912)

PRAYER

Frost has stretched a stern hand over my garden
Locking in icy grip all growth for a season,
Binding motions of earth in a hard dominion
     And brittle quiet.

Were it not well, O Lord, to stretch forth thy finger
Firmer than frost over these thy quarrelsome children,
Staying their strife with a sleep not soon to be broken,
     Staying Earth, their mother?

Sleep from a fairy tale, Lord, seizing factories in motion,
Airplanes poised in the blue like dragonflies dormant,
Rifles, bombs, tanks, cannon, warships, armies embattled
     Conquered by silence.

When they awake O let them rub eyes of wonder,
Stare with amaze at the countless engines of malice,
Loose in their hearts a joy never known to destruction,
     Let them find wisdom.

C. COLLEER ABBOTT

THOUGHTS IN A GARDEN

How vain themselves amaze
To win the palm, the oak, or bays,
And their uncessant labours see
Crown'd from single herb or tree,
Whose short and narrow-vergèd shade
Does prudently their toils upbraid;
While all the flowers and trees do close
To weave the garlands of repose!

Fair Quiet, have I found thee here,
And Innocence thy sister dear?
Mistaken long, I sought you then
In busy companies of men:
Your sacred plants, if here below,
Only among the plants will grow:
Society is all but rude
To this delicious solitude.

No white nor red was ever seen
So amorous as this lovely green.
Fond lovers, cruel as their flame,
Cut in these trees their mistress' name:
Little, alas! they know or heed
How far these beauties her exceed!
Fair trees! wheres'e'er your barks I wound,
No name shall but your own be found.

When we have run our passions' heat,
Love hither makes his best retreat:
The gods, that mortal beauty chase,
Still in a tree did end their race;
Apollo hunted Daphne so
Only that she might laurel grow;
And Pan did after Syrinx speed
Not as a nymph, but for a reed.

What a wondrous life is this I lead!
Ripe apples drop about my head;
The luscious clusters of the vine
Upon my mouth do crush their wine;
The nectarine and curious peach
Into my hands themselves do reach;
Stumbling on melons, as I pass,
Ensnared with flowers, I fall on grass.

Meanwhile the mind from pleasure less
Withdraws into its happiness;
The mind, that Ocean where each kind
Does straight its own resemblance find;
Yet it creates, transcending these,
Far other worlds, and other seas;
Annihilating all that's made
To a green thought in a green shade.

Here at the fountain's sliding foot,
Or at some fruit-tree's mossy root,
Casting the body's vest aside,
My soul into the boughs does glide;
There, like a bird, it sits and sings,
Then whets and combs its silver wings,
And, till prepared for longer flight,
Waves in its plumes the various light.

Such was that happy Garden-state
While man there walk'd without a mate:
After a place so pure and sweet,
What other help could yet be meet!
But 'twas beyond a mortal's share
To wander solitary there:
Two paradises 'twere in one,
To live in Paradise alone.

How well the skilful gard'ner drew
Of flowers and herbs this dial new!
Where, from above, the milder sun
Does through a fragrant zodiac run:
And, as it works, th' industrious bee
Computes its time as well as we.
How could such sweet and wholesome hours
Be reckon'd, but with herbs and flowers!

ANDREW MARVELL (1621–1678)

A LETTER TO SIR THOMAS BROWNE

Co. Garden, Lond. 28 Jan. (1657–8)

Sir, I return you a thousand acknowledgements for the papers which you transmitted me, and will render you this account of my present undertaking. The truth is, that which imported me to discourse on this subject after this sort was the many defects which I encountered in books and in gardens, wherein neither words nor cost had been wanting, but judgement very much; and though I cannot boast of my science in this kind, as both unbecoming my years and my small experience, yet I esteemed it pardonable at least, if in doing my endeavour to rectify some mistakes, and advancing so useful and innocent a divertisement, I made some essay, and cast in my symbol with the rest . . .

The model, which I perceive you have seen, will abundantly testify my abhorrency of those painted and formal projections of our cockney gardens and plots, which appear like gardens of paste-board and marchpane, and smell more of paint than of flowers and verdure: our drift is a noble, princely, and universal Elysium, capable of all the amenities that can naturally be introduced into gardens of pleasure, and such as may stand in competition with all the august designs and stories of this nature, either of ancient or modern times; yet so as to become useful and significant to the least pretences and faculties.

We will endeavour to show how the air and genius of gardens operate upon human spirits towards virtue and sanctity, I mean in a remote, preparatory, and instrumental working, how caves, grots, mounts, and irregular ornaments of gardens do contribute to contemplative and philosophical enthusiasm; how elysium, antrum, nemus, paradysus, hortus, lucus, &c., signify all of them rem sacram et divinam; for these expedients do influence the soul and spirits of man, and prepare them for converse with good angels; besides which, they contribute to the less abstracted pleasures, philosophy natural and longevity; and I would have not only the eulogies and effigy of the ancient and famous garden heroes, but a society of the paradisi cultores, persons of ancient simplicity, Paradisean and Hortulan saints, to be a society of learned and ingenuous men, such as Dr. Browne, by whom we might hope to redeem the time that has been lost in pursuing Vulgar Errours and still propagating them, as so many bad men do yet presume to do.

Were it to be hoped, inter hos armorum strepitus, and in so general a catalysis of integrity, interruption of peace and propriety, the hortulan pleasures, these innocent, pure, and useful diversions might enjoy the least encouragement, whilst brutish and ambitious persons seek themselves in the ruins of our miserable yet dearest country, quis talia fando – ?

JOHN EVELYN (1620–1706)

28

I thank God this sort of diversion has tended very much to the ease and quiet of my one Mind; and the Retirement I find therein, by Walking and Meditation, has help'd to set foward many useful thoughts upon more divine Subjects . . . In the meantime I cannot but encourage and invite my reverend Brethren to the love of a Garden; having myself all along reaped so much Fruit from it, both in a figurative and literal sense.

JOHN LAWRENCE
The Clergyman's Recreation (1714)

GARDENS AND THE RELIGIOUS

Our saxon ancestors certainly had some sort of cabbage, because they call the month of February Sproutcale; but long after their days, the cultivation of gardens was little attended to.

The religious, being men of leisure, and keeping up a constant correspondence with Italy, were the first people among us that had gardens and fruit-trees in any perfection, within the walls of their abbeys, priories and monasteries, where the lamp of knowledge continued to burn, however dimly. In them men of business were formed for the state: the art of writing was cultivated by the monks; they were the only proficients in mechanics, gardening, and architecture. The barons neglected every pursuit that did not lead to war, or tend to the pleasure of the chase.

It was not till gentlemen took up the study of horticulture themselves, that the knowledge of gardening made such hasty advances. Lord Cobham, Lord Ila, and Mr. Waller of Beaconsfield, were some of the first people of rank that promoted the elegant science of ornamenting without despising the superintendence of the kitchen quarters and fruit walls.

GILBERT WHITE (1720–1793)
The Natural History of Selborne

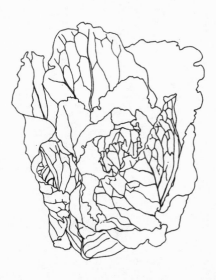

To Grimwold, Abbot of St Gall,
with his book *Of Gardening*

A very paltry gift, of no account,
My father, for a scholar like to thee,
But Strabo sends it to thee with his heart.
So might you sit in the small garden close
In the green darkness of the apple trees
Just where the peach tree casts its broken shade,
And they would gather you the shining fruit
With the soft down upon it; all your boys,
Your little laughing boys, your happy school,
And bring huge apples clasped in their two hands.
Something the book may have of use to thee.
Read it, my father, prune it of its faults,
And strengthen with thy praise what pleases thee.
And may God give thee in thy hands the green
Unwithering palm of everlasting life.

WALAFRID STRABO (809–849)

PARADISE

And the Lord God planted a garden eastward in Eden; and there he put the man whom he had formed. And out of the ground made the Lord God to grow every tree that is pleasant to the sight, and good for food; the tree of life also in the midst of the garden, and the tree of knowledge of good and evil. And a river went out of Eden to water the garden; and from thence it was parted, and became four heads. The name of the first is Pison: that is it which compasseth the whole land of Havilah, where there is gold; and the gold of that land is good: there is bdellium and the onyx stone. And the name of the second river is Gihon: the same is it that compasseth the whole land of Ethiopia. And the name of the third river is Hiddekel: that is it which goeth toward the east of Assyria. And the fourth river is Euphrates. And the Lord God took the man, and put him into the garden of Eden to dress it and to keep it. And the Lord God commanded the man, saying, Of every tree of the garden thou mayest freely eat: but of the tree of the knowledge of good and evil, thou shalt not eat of it: for in the day that thou eatest thereof thou shalt surely die . . .

. . . Now the serpent was more subtil than any beast of the field which the Lord God had made. And he said unto the woman, Yea hath God said, Ye shall not eat of every tree of the garden? And the woman said unto the serpent, We may eat of the fruit of the trees of the garden: but of the fruit of the tree which is in the midst of the garden, God hath said, Ye shall not eat of it, neither shall ye touch it, lest ye die. And the serpent said unto the woman, Ye shall not surely die: for God doth know that in the day ye eat thereof, then your eyes shall be opened, and ye shall be as gods, knowing good and evil. And when the woman saw that the tree was good for food, and that it was pleasant to the eyes, and a tree to be desired to make one wise, she took of the fruit thereof, and did eat, and gave also unto her husband with her; and he did eat. And the eyes of them both were opened, and they knew that they were naked; and they sewed fig leaves together, and themselves aprons. And they heard the voice of the Lord God amongst the trees of the garden. And the Lord God called unto Adam, and said unto him, Where art thou? . . .

. . . And unto Adam he said, Because thou hast hearkened
unto the voice of thy wife, and hast eaten of the tree, of which I
commanded thee, saying, Thou shalt not eat of it; thorns also and
thistles shall it bring forth to thee; and thou shalt eat the herb of the
field; in the sweat of thy face shalt thou eat bread, till thou return
unto the ground; for out of it wast thou taken: for dust thou art,
and unto dust shalt thou return . . .

Genesis 2:8–17; 3:1–9, 17–19

34

And God said, Behold, I have given you every herb bearing seed, which is upon the face of all the earth, and every tree, in the which is the fruit of a tree yielding seed; to you it shall be for meat. And to every beast of the earth, and to every fowl of the air, and to every thing that creepeth upon the earth, wherein there is life, I have given every green herb for meat: and it was so . . .

Genesis 1:29–30

EDEN

        In this pleasant soile
His farre more pleasant Garden God ordained;
Out of the fertile ground he caus'd to grow
All Trees of noblest kind for sight, smell, taste;
And all amid them stood the Tree of Life,
High, eminent, blooming Ambrosial Fruit
Of vegetable Gold; and next to Life
Our Death the Tree of Knowledge grew fast by . . .
                        Thus was this place,
A happy rural seat of various view:
Groves whose rich Trees wept odorous Gumms and Balme,
Others whose fruit burnisht with Golden Rind
Hung amiable, Hesperian Fables true,
If true, here onely, and of delicious taste:
Betwixt them Lawns, or level Downs, and Flocks
Grasing the tender herb, were interpos'd,
Or palmie hilloc, or the flourie lap
Of som irriguous Valley spread her store,
Flours of all hue, and without Thorn the Rose;
Another side, umbrageous Grots and Caves
Of coole recess, o're which the mantling Vine
Layes forth her purple Grape, and gently creeps;
Luxuriant; mean while murmuring waters fall
Down the slope hills, disperst, or in a Lake,
That to the fringed Bank with Myrtle crown'd,
Her chrystall mirror holds, unite their streams,
The Birds their quire apply; aires, vernal aires,
Breathing the smell of field and grove, attune,
The trembling leaves, while Universal Pan
Knit with the Graces and the Hours in dance
Led on th' Eternal Spring.

JOHN MILTON (1608–1674)

Oh that I was the bird of Paradise!
        Then in thy nutmeg garden, Lord, thy bower,
Celestial music blossom should my voice,
        Enchanted with thy garden's air and flower.
        This aromatic air would so inspire
        My ravish'd soul to sing with angels' choir.

What is thy church, my Lord, thy garden which
        Doth gain the best of soils? Such spots indeed
Are choicest plots empal'd with palings rich
        And set with slips, herbs best, and best of seed,
        As th' Hanging Gardens rare of Babylon
        And palace garden of King Solomon.

But that which doth excel all gardens here
        Was Eden's garden, Adam's palace bright.
The Tree of Life, and Knowledge too, were there,
        Sweet herbs and sweetest flowers, all sweet delight,
        A Paradise indeed of all perfume
        That to the nose, the eyes and ears doth tune.

But all these artificial gardens bright
        Enamelèd with bravest knots of pinks
And flowers enspangled with black, red and white,
        Compar'd with this are truly stinking sinks.
        As dunghills reek with stinking scents that dish
        Us out, so these, when balancèd with this.

For Zion's Paradise, Christ's garden dear,
        His church, enwalled with heavenly crystal fine,
Hath every bed beset with pearl all clear
        And alleys opal'd with gold, and silver shrine.
        The shining angels are its sentinels
        With flaming sword chanting out madrigals.

The sparkling plants, sweet spices, herbs and trees,
        The glorious shows of aromatic flowers,
The pleasing beauties soak'd in sweet breath lees
        Of Christ's rich garden ever upward towers.
        For Christ sweet showers of Grace makes on it fall.
        It therefore bears the bell away from all.

The nut of ev'ry kind is found to grow big
       With food, and physic, lodg'd within a tower,
A wooden wall with husky coverlid
       Or shell flesh'd o'er, or in an arching bower:
       Beech, hazel, walnut, cocho, almond brave,
       Pistick or chestnut in its prickly cave.

These all as meat and med'cine, emblems choice
       Of spiritual food and physic are, which sport
Up in Christ's garden. Yet the nutmeg's spice
       A leathern coat wears, and a macy shirt,
       Doth far excel them all. Aromatize
       My soul therewith, my Lord, and spiritual-wise.

Oh sweet, sweet Paradise, whose spicèd spring
       Will make the lips of him asleep to tune
Heart-ravishing tunes, sweet music for our king
       In aromatic air of blest perfume,
       Open thy garden door. Me entrance give,
       And in thy nut-tree garden make me live.

If, Lord, thou ope'st, and in thy garden bring
       Me, then thy linnet sweetly will
Upon thy nut-tree sit and sweetly sing,
       Will crack a nut and eat the kernel still.
       Thou wilt mine eyes, my nose and palate greet
       With curious flowers, sweet odours, viands sweet.

Thy garden's odiferous air me make
       Suck in and out, to aromatize my lungs,
That I thy garden and its spicy state
       May breathe upon with such ensweetened songs,
       My lungs and breath ensweetened thus shall raise
       The glory of thy garden in its praise.

EDWARD TAYLOR (?1642–1729)
Preparatory Meditations Before My Approach to the Lord's Supper Meditation.
Canticles 6:11 'I went down into the Garden of Nuts, to see the fruits' etc

PROOF OF PARADISE

Grandfather and Bates and the Old Man ambled along in the governess cart through the wood discussing gooseberries and the devil. They went slowly because the Old Man, being nearly as tall as the giant in the fairy tale who carried his heart in a paper bag, weighed down the governess cart very heavily. The subject of gooseberries had come up because in observing each other's rheumaticky hands Grandfather and the Old Man had realized that they both suffered from the same complaint, so aggravated by the eating of gooseberry pie.

'The nicest kind of pie there is too,' grumbled Grandfather. 'Abstention from it is a real penance to me.'

'You 'as a nice baked apple on gooseberry days,' Bates reproved him. 'I grows the apples special.'

Grandfather accepted the reproof with humility. 'So I do, Bates. And what could be nicer than a baked apple? A beautiful fruit, the apple, and always with us. It grew in the Garden of Eden. It grew in the Garden of the Hesperides. I do not doubt that we shall find apple trees growing in the Garden of Paradise; Blenheim Oranges, one trusts.'

'I'm more partial to a Cox's Pippin meself,' said Bates. 'Or a Newton Wonder. A beautiful apple, the Newton Wonder.'

The Old Man was busy putting finishing touches to the two wax images with the pins stuck in them. He had given an eye-glass to the larger figure and a rather impudent expression to the smaller. Now he looked up and spoke. 'Speakin' for meself, I'm more partial to a nice radish,' he said. 'More tasty, like. An' as for the Garden of paradise – there ain't no Paradise.'

'What?' cried Grandfather in horror and indignation. 'My dear sir! My dear sir!' And he pulled Albert [the pony] to a standstill to argue the point. 'No Paradise? Have you no eyes, no ears? Have you not seen flowers growing, heard birds singing? Have you no heart to feel these things? Where do you keep your heart, my dear sir? In a paper bag? Good heavens! Dear me! Do you not realize that these beauties are shouting aloud the promise of the joy to come? No deafness, not even yours, my dear sir, is an excuse for not hearing. They shout so loud about it that one might almost say they are the joy to come. Paradise is already present in this world, my dear sir, even as March daffodils dancing in the wind are present in the green shoots of February . . . Dear me!' said Grandfather, removing his hat and mopping his brow. 'I dislike preaching a sermon in a heat wave, but I am driven to it by the horror of your views. No Paradise!'

"Is own garden's in a shockin' mess," said Bates, as though this explained the Old Man's deplorable lack of faith. "'E's not taken a spade to that garden for twenty year or more."

ELIZABETH GOUDGE (1900–1984)
Henrietta's House

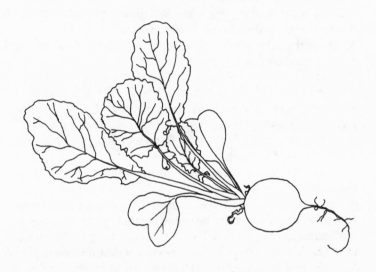

40

To come back sometimes, that is all I ask,
To smooth the soil, to count the roses, dip
My fingers in the stream, see if the beasts
Still know me, and to recollect the names
That Adam gave them (Do they live there still?
They must, they must)

           – Even to go back once,
To bear my first child there, hearing the leaves,
To lie exhausted on familiar grass,
Wait for the cool of evening when he walks
Among the trees: then I would call him over,
And hold the baby in my tired arms,
And say, God bless it.

           That is all I ask.

Adam explained, explained: 'We can't go back.
That is our punishment.'

           But even if
I'm not allowed to touch, just to be there,
To smell the grass, the damp, the honeysuckle,
The rain –

           And if I'm not allowed to smell,
To see the shades of green, the yellowing leaves
Curl in the sun,

           – even to shut my eyes
And hear it all continue, hear the hum,
The growl of life –

Adam explained again: 'There's nothing there.'

There must be, Adam. They were innocent,
The creatures. Creeping, flying, running,
Dependent on each other and the sun,
Not needing us, not hurt by us, not us.
It can't be, can't be, God is just. And even –
Even if not, if God is selfish, still
He walked there in the evening, he loved that,
He'd keep it, for his pleasure –

           'God? He'll manage.'

What can I dream of, Adam, if not that?
To wake and find you there, the fruit uneaten,
The four streams flowing to an unknown world,
The creatures friendly, and the snake with legs:
What else, what else?

Dreaming is still allowed.
Perhaps he can't prevent us. Now it's gone,
Now nothing's there, all dreams are possible.

LAURENCE LERNER

My Garden

A garden is a lovesome thing, God wot!
        Rose plot,
        Fringed pool,
Fern'd grot –
        The veriest school
        Of peace; and yet the fool
Contends that God is not –
Not God! in gardens! when the eve is cool?
        Nay, but I have a sign;
        'Tis very sure God walks in mine.

T.E. BROWN (1830–1897)

GARDENS FAR
IN SPACE AND TIME

To Western minds the word 'garden' suggests primarily a garden of flowers, but the records show that the gardens of the oldest civilizations were gardens of trees and scented shrubs. Shade, scent and water were the chief requisites in the gardens of the ancient East, water being the soul of the Eastern paradise and shade the essential luxury. The mystic garden of Eden was a true Eastern paradise – a garden of trees and of living waters. The record in Genesis makes no mention of flowers. 'And out of the ground made the Lord God to grow every tree that is pleasant to the sight and good for food . . . and a river went out of Eden to water the garden.'

Throughout the Bible greater importance is attached to trees than to flowers and they are more frequently mentioned than flowers. Reference may be made to Jotham's parable of the trees (Judges 9:8), Nebuchadnezzar's dream (Daniel 4:10), and to the laws concerning trees (Leviticus 19:23, 27:30, Deuteronomy 20:19).

Of the glory of the King of Assyria Ezekiel says, 'The cedars in the garden of God could not hide him, the fir trees were not like his boughs, and the chestnut trees were not like his branches; nor any tree in the Garden of Eden was like unto him in his beauty . . . all the trees of Eden, that were in the garden of God envied him' (Ezekiel 31:8,9).

The ancient Egyptian made a garden not only for his enjoyment in this life, but also that after death his soul might come out of the tomb in the cool of the evening and enjoy the shade. In Genesis we find that God Himself deigned to walk 'in the cool of the day' in the shade of the trees He had planted.

ELEANOUR SINCLAIR RHODE
Garden-Craft in the Bible

THE GARDEN OF LOVE

I am the rose of Sharon,
And the lily of the valleys.
As the lily among thorns,
So is my love among the daughters.
As the apple tree among the trees of the wood,
So is my beloved among the sons.
I sat down under his shadow with great delight,
And his fruit was sweet to my taste.
He brought me to the banqueting house,
And his banner over me was love.
Stay me with flagons, comfort me with apples . . .
A garden inclosed is my sister, my spouse;
A spring shut up, a fountain sealed.
Thy plants are an orchard of pomegranates, with pleasant fruits;
Camphire, with spikenard,
Spikenard and saffron;
Calamus and cinnamon, with all trees of frankincense;
Myrrh and aloes, with all the chief spices:
A fountain of gardens,
A well of living waters,
And streams from Lebanon.
Awake, O north wind; and come, thou south;
Blow upon my garden, that the spices thereof may flow out.
Let my beloved come into his garden,
And eat his pleasant fruits.
I am come into my garden, my sister, my spouse:
I have gathered my myrrh with my spice;
I have eaten my honeycomb with my honey;
I have drunk my wine with my milk:
Eat, O friends;
Drink, yea, drink abundantly, O beloved . . .
Come, my beloved, let us go forth into the field;
Let us lodge in the villages.
Let us get up early to the vineyards;
Let us see if the vine flourish, whether the tender grape appear,
And the pomegranates bud forth:
There will I give thee my loves.
The mandrakes give a smell,
And at our gates are all manner of pleasant fruits, new and old,
Which I have laid up for thee, O my beloved.

Song of Solomon 2:1–5; 4:12–5:1; 7:11–13

He gave us this eternal Spring,
Which here enamels every thing;
And sends the Fowls to us in care,
On daily Visits through the Air.
He hangs in shades the Orange bright,
Like golden Lamps in a green Night,
And does in the Pomegranates close
Jewels more rich than Ormus shows.
He makes the Figs our mouths to meet,
And throws the Melons at our feet;
But Apples plants of such a price,
No tree could ever bear them twice.
With Cedars, chosen by his hand
From Lebanon, he stores the Land . . .

ANDREW MARVELL (1621–1678)
Bermudas

THE JAPANESE GARDEN

No effort to create an impossible or purely ideal landscape is made in the Japanese garden. Its artistic purpose is to copy faithfully the attractions of a veritable landscape, and to convey the real impression that a real landscape communicates. It is therefore at once a picture and a poem; perhaps even more a poem than a picture. For as nature's scenery, in its varying aspects, affects us with sensations of joy or of solemnity, of grimness or of sweetness, of force or of peace, so must the true reflection of it in the labour of the landscape gardener create not merely an impression of beauty, but a mood in the soul. The grand old landscape gardeners, those Buddhist monks who first introduced the art into Japan, and subsequently developed it into an almost occult science, carried their theory yet farther than this. They held it possible to express moral lessons in the design of a garden, and abstract ideas, such as Chastity, Faith, Piety, Content, Calm, and Connubial Bliss. Therefore were gardens contrived according to the character of the owner, whether poet, warrior, philosopher, or priest. In those ancient gardens (the art, alas, is passing away under the withering influence of the utterly commonplace Western taste) there were expressed both a mood of nature and some rare Oriental conception of a mood of man.

LAFCADIO HEARN (1850–1904)
Glimpses of Unfamiliar Japan

I am always happy (out of doors be it understood, for indoors there are servants and furniture), but in quite different ways, and my spring happiness bears no resemblance to my summer and autumn happiness, though it is not more intense, and there were days last winter when I danced for sheer joy out in my frost-bound garden in spite of my years and children. But I did it behind a bush, having a due regard for the decencies.

There are so many bird-cherries round me, great trees with branches sweeping the grass, and they are so wreathed just now with white blossoms and tenderest green that the garden looks like a wedding. I never saw such masses of them; they seem to fill the place. Even across a little stream that bounds the garden on the east, and right in the middle of the cornfield beyond, there is an immense one, a picture of grace and glory against the cold blue of the spring sky.

My garden is surrounded by cornfields and meadows, and beyond are great stretches of sandy heath and pine forests, and where the forests leave off the bare heath begins again; but the forests are beautiful in their lofty, pink-stemmed vastness, far overhead the crowns of softest grey-green, and underfoot a bright green whortleberry carpet, and everywhere the breathless silence; and the bare heaths are beautiful too, for one can see across them into eternity almost, and to go out on to them with one's face towards the setting sun is like going into the very presence of God . . .

. . . The garden is the place I go to for refuge and shelter, not the house. In the house are duties and annoyances, servants to exhort and admonish, furniture, and meals; but out there blessings crowd round me at every step – it is there that I am sorry for the unkindness in me, for those selfish thoughts that are so much worse than they feel, it is there that all my sins and silliness are forgiven, there that I feel protected and at home, and every flower and weed is a friend and every tree a lover. When I have been vexed I run out to them for comfort, and when I have been angry without just cause, it is there that I find absolution. Did ever a woman have so many friends? And always the same, always ready to welcome me and fill me with cheerful thoughts. Happy children of a common Father, why should I, their own sister, be less content and joyous than they?

ELIZABETH VON ARNIM (1866–1941)
Elizabeth and her German Garden

LORD JESUS
HATH A GARDEN

CHRIST, MY BELOVED

Christ, my Beloved which still doth feed
  Among the flowers, having delight
  Among his faithful lilies,
Doth take great care for me indeed,
  And I again with all my might
  Will do what so his will is.

My Love in me and I in him,
  Conjoined by love, will still abide
  Among the faithful lilies
Till day do break, and truth do dim
  All shadows dark and cause them slide,
  According as his will is.

WILLIAM BALDWIN (fl. 1547–1549)

THE GARDEN OF JESUS

Lord Jesus hath a garden, full of flowers gay,
Where you and I can gather nosegays all the day:

> *There angels sing in jubilant ring,*
> *With dulcimers and lutes,*
> *And harps, and cymbals, trumpets, pipes,*
> *And gentle, soothing flutes.*

There bloometh white the lily, flower of Purity;
The fragrant violet hides there, sweet Humility:

The rose's name is Patience, pruned to greater might;
The marigold's, Obedience, plentiful and bright:

And Hope and Faith are there; but of these three the best,
Is Love, whose crown-imperial spreads o'er all the rest:

And one thing fairest is in all that lovely maze,
The gardener, Jesus Christ, whom all the flowers praise:

O Jesus, all my good and my bliss! Ah me!
Thy garden make my heart, which ready is for thee!

Dutch carol

Lily Violet Rose & Marigold

We are a Garden wall'd around,
Chosen and made peculiar Ground;
A little Spot inclos'd by Grace
Out of the World's wide Wilderness.

Like Trees of Myrrh and Spice we stand,
Planted by God the Father's Hand;
And all his Springs in Sion flow,
To make the young Plantation grow.

Awake, O heavenly Wind, and come,
Blow on this garden of Perfume;
Spirit Divine, descend and breathe
A gracious Gale on Plants beneath.

Make our best Spices flow abroad
To entertain our Saviour-God:
And Faith, and Love, and Joy appear,
And every Grace be active here.

Let my Beloved come, and taste
His pleasant Fruits at his own Feast.
I come, my Spouse, I come, he cries,
With Love and Pleasure in his eyes.

Our Lord into his Garden comes,
Well pleas'd to smell our poor Perfumes,
And calls us to a Feast divine,
Sweeter than Honey, Milk, or Wine.

Eat of the tree of Life, my Friends,
The Blessings that my Father sends;
Your taste shall all my Dainties prove,
And drink abundance of my Love.

Jesus, we will frequent thy board,
And sing the Bounties of our Lord:
But the rich Food on which we live
Demands more Praise than Tongues can give.

ISAAC WAATS (1674–1748)

KINDLY SPRING AGAIN IS HERE

Kindly spring again is here,
Trees and fields in bloom appear;
Hark! the birds with artless lays
Warble their creator's praise.

Where in winter all was snow,
Now the flowers in clusters grow;
And the corn, in green array,
Promises a harvest-day.

Lord, afford a spring to me,
Let me feel like what I see;
Speak, and by thy gracious voice,
Make my drooping soul rejoice.

On thy garden deign to smile,
Raise the plants, enrich the soil;
Soon thy presence will restore
Life to what seemed dead before.

JOHN NEWTON (1725–1807)

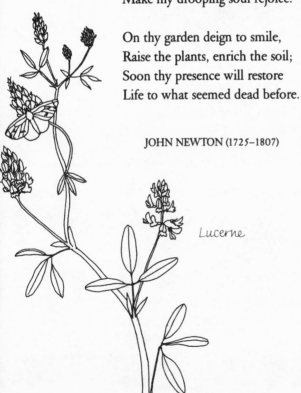

Lucerne

54   When Jesus had spoken these words, he went forth with his
       disciples over the brook Cedron, where was a garden, into the which
       he entered, and his disciples. And Judas also, which betrayed him,
       knew the place: for Jesus ofttimes resorted thither with his disciples.

John 18:1–2

Now in the place where he was crucified there was a garden; and in the garden a new sepulchre, wherein was never man yet laid. There laid they Jesus . . .

But Mary stood without at the sepulchre weeping: and as she wept, she stooped down, and looked into the sepulchre, and seeth two angels in white sitting, the one at the head, and the other at the feet, where the body of Jesus had lain. And they say unto her, Woman, why weepest thou? She saith unto them, Because they have taken away my Lord, and I know not where they have laid him. And when she had thus said, she turned herself back, and saw Jesus standing, and knew not that it was Jesus. Jesus saith unto her, Woman, why weepest thou? whom seekest thou? She, supposing him to be the gardener, saith unto him, Sir, if thou have borne him hence, tell me where thou hast laid him, and I will take him away. Jesus saith unto her, Mary. She turned herself, and saith unto him, Rabboni; which is to say, Master . . .

John 19:41; 20:11–16

Spring has now unwrapped the flowers,
    Day is fast reviving,
Life in all her growing powers
    Towards the light is striving:
Gone the iron touch of cold,
    Winter time and frost time,
Seedlings, working the mould,
    Now make up for lost time.

Herb and plant that, winter long,
    Slumbered at their leisure,
Now bestirring, green and strong,
    Find in growth their pleasure:
All the world with beauty fills,
    Gold the green enhancing;
Flowers make merry on the hills,
    Set the meadows dancing.

Through each wonder of fair days
    God himself expresses;
Beauty follows all his ways,
    As the world he blesses:
So, as he renews the earth,
    Artist without rival,
In his grace of glad new birth
    We must seek revival.

Earth is garbed in revelry,
    Flowers and grasses hide her;
We go forth in charity –
    Brothers all beside her;
For, as man this glory sees
    In the awakening season,
Reason learns the heart's decrees,
    Hearts are led by reason.

Praise the Maker, all ye saints;
        He with glory girt you,
He who skies and meadows paints
        Fashioned all your virtue;
Praise him, seers, heroes, kings,
        Heralds of perfection;
Brothers, praise him, for he brings
        All to resurrection!

ANONYMOUS

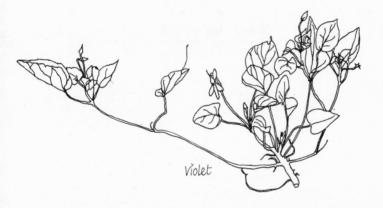

Violet

EASTER

I got me flowers to straw Thy way,
    I got me boughs off many a tree;
But Thou wast up by break of day,
    And brought'st Thy sweets along with Thee.

Yet though my flowers be lost, they say
    A heart can never come too late;
Teach it to sing Thy praise this day,
    And then this day my life shall date.

GEORGE HERBERT (1593–1633)
This is a synthesis of two different versions of the poem.

A CHAPTER OF SAINTS

St Phocas was a humble market gardener of the third century who lived near the city gate of Sinope in Pontus, by the southern shores of the Black Sea. He grew fruit and vegetables for the markets and herbs for the poor, dedicating his life to prayer and work. During a spate of persecutions, he was suspected of being a Christian and two soldiers were deputed to find and execute him. They drew near to Sinope as night was falling, and, seeing the cottage and garden, stopped to beg food and shelter for the night. Phocas was so generous and hospitable in his welcome that they confided their mission to him. He betrayed no fear, but simply told them that he knew the man they were looking for, and that he would fetch him in the morning.

When the soldiers were asleep, Phocas dug himself a grave in his own beloved garden, and then gave himself up to prayer. When dawn came, he woke the soldiers and, to their horror and dismay, gave himself up to them. Nevertheless, they carried out their orders. He was executed, and buried in the grave dug amongst his own flowers. Later, a church was built over that place, and St Phocas became the patron saint of gardeners.

St Fiacre is another saint venerated by gardeners. Legend has it, he grew the most splendid vegetables in his hermitage garden in the forest of Breuil. He was born in Ireland in the seventh century, but turning his back on his family's wealth and position, he went to France and asked Faro, the Bishop of Meaux, to allow him to lead the life of a hermit.

When he was given his clearing, a fence was heard to have been miraculously placed round the garden, which story was told to Faro by a woman who denounced the miracle as the devil's work. The bishop was satisfied that this was not true, and one wonders quite what happened to the woman for, after this, no woman ever dared to approach the garden on pain of going blind. And later, when a chapel in the cathedral of Meaux was consecrated to the saint, women still refused to enter it.

St Clare was a gardener: she grew her favourite flowers – violets, lilies and roses – outside the convent at San Damiano. So too was St Adalhardt, a monk at Corbie in France, of whom it was said, 'With Mary he sought Jesus in the garden.' St Radegund and Venantius Fortunatus, Bishop of Poitiers, were both inspired by flowers. He would send her flowers, and we have a note which accompanied a bunch of his sixth-century violets which reads:

He who offers violets must in love be held to offer roses. Of all the fragrant herbs I send none can compare in nobleness with the purple violet. They shine in royal purple: perfume and beauty unite in their petals. May you show forth in your life what they represent.

Serenus was a fourth-century Greek who settled in a hermitage in Hungary and cultivated a beautiful garden. That garden was his undoing, for it was there that a woman made an assignation with her lover. Serenus chased her away and she complained of his rudeness to her husband who was one of the emperor's officers. In the ensuing row, the truth came out, and the charges against Serenus were dropped, but the governor of the province began to suspect that Serenus was a Christian and he was martyred.

Maurilius' fondness for gardening is not well-documented. We know for certain that he was Milanese and eventually became the Bishop of Angers in the fourth century. But the story goes that he became a gardener to an English lord, having run away from Angers in a seizure of remorse for postponing a dying boy's baptism until too late. While on board ship, he threw the cathedral keys into the sea, and vowed that he would never return without them.

His time as a gardener may well have been one of unrelieved misery, but the story ends happily, however, for his flock sought him out and a fish turned up at the table with the cathedral keys in its stomach. It would be straining at gnats to arrive thus far and then not to credit the end of the story. When Maurilius was enthroned once more, he went to the grave of the poor, unbaptized boy and prayed for a while. The boy was resurrected and christened 'Renatus'. (And he became the Bishop of Sorrento.)

Elizabeth of Hungary was no gardener, far from it! Yet her emblem is a basket of roses. She was a queen with an unusual propensity for giving away to the poor anything on which she could lay her hands. This annoyed her husband, Ludwig, so much that he scolded her for her charities. One day, when he was out hunting, he met her carrying bread to the poor, and demanded to know what was in her basket. But when she, frightened and ashamed, pulled off the napkin to show the bread inside, there was nothing but roses.

St Dorothy, too, has a basket of roses, and fruit as well, for her symbol. The story goes that she was a beautiful girl living in Caesarea in Cappadocia, during the time of the Diocletian persecutions. She resisted all attempts to make her give up her faith and was sentenced to death. As she was led to her execution, Theophilus, a lawyer, asked sneeringly if she would send him some flowers and fruit from the heavenly garden. Suddenly, a child appeared, carrying a basket of roses and apples, which Dorothy immediately sent to Theophilus. He was converted and, almost as soon, martyred.

Thérèse of Lisieux – the Little Flower of Jesus as she delighted to call herself – is the last and most modern saint who is particularly associated with flowers. She wrote 'To strew flowers is the only means of proving my love, and these flowers will be each word and look, each daily sacrifice.' She faced an early death from tuberculosis, but before she died she wrote 'I will spend my Heaven in doing good upon earth . . . I will let fall a shower of roses.' Perhaps the 'shower of roses' are the miracles which have been attributed to her and led eventually to her canonization in 1925.

F.M.

OUR LADY'S FLOWERS

Foxglove

Lily of the Valley

Fuschia

Lady's Smock

Kidney Vetch

Harebell

Meadowsweet

Lungwort

Ribbongrass

Bird's Foot Trefoil

Parsley

Ground Ivy

Dodder

Alchemilla

Specularia hybridis

weed

Thrift

Our Lady's:

Nightcap	Convolvulus
Hair	Wild orchis
Tears	Lungwort; Lily of the valley
Eardrops	Fuschia
Smock	Cuckoo flowers
Fingers	Kidney vetch
Thimble	Harebell
Gloves	Foxgloves
Girdle	Meadowsweet
Garters	Ribbongrass
Slipper	Bird's foot trefoil
Laces	Strangleweed
Mantle	Alchemilla
Looking-glass	*Specularia bybridia*
Comb	*Scandix pecten-veneris*
Keys	Primrose
Cushion	Thrift
Purse	Portacula
Candlestick	Primula
Virgin's bower	Wild clematis
Herb of the Madonna	Ground ivy
Our Lady's little vine	Parsley

64

Jerusalem, my happy home,
　　　　When shall I came to thee?
When shall my sorrows have an end?
　　　　Thy joys when shall I see?

O happy harbour of the saints!
　　　　O sweet and pleasant soil!
In thee no sorrow may be found,
　　　　No grief, no care, no toil . . .

No dampish mist is seen in thee,
　　　　No cold nor darksome night;
There every soul shines as the sun;
　　　　There God himself gives light . . .

Thy vineyards and thy orchards are
　　　　Most beautiful and fair,
Full furnishèd with trees and fruits,
　　　　Most wonderful and rare;

Thy gardens and thy gallant walks
　　　　Continually are green;
There grow such sweet and pleasant flowers
　　　　As nowhere else are seen.

There's nectar and ambrosia made,
　　　　There's musk and civet sweet;
There many a fair and dainty drug
　　　　Is trodden under feet.

There cinnamon, there sugar grows,
　　　　There nard and balm abound:
What tongue can tell, or heart conceive,
　　　　The joys that there are found!

Quite through the streets with silver sound
　　　　The flood of life do flow,
Upon whose banks on every side
　　　　The wood of life doth grow.

There trees for evermore bear fruit,
　　　　And evermore do spring;
There evermore the angels sit,
　　　　And evermore do sing.

There David stands with harp in hand
　　　　As master of the choir:
Ten thousand times that man were blest
　　　　That might this music hear.

Our Lady sings Magnificat
　　　　With tune surpassing sweet;
And all the virgins bear their parts,
　　　　Sitting about her feet.

Te Deum doth Saint Ambrose sing,
　　　　Saint Austin doth the like;
Old Simeon and Zachary
　　　　Have not their songs to seek.

There Magdalene hath left her moan,
　　　　And cheerfully doth sing
With blessed saints, whose harmony
　　　　In every street doth ring.

Jerusalem, my happy home,
　　　　Would God I were in thee!
Would God my woes were at an end,
　　　　Thy joys that I might see!

ANONYMOUS (c. 1600)

A Calendar of Saints and their Flowers

4 December	Barbara	Herb St Barbara (winter cress)
29 December	St Thomas à Becket	Canterbury bells
1 January	Faine	Viburnum
13 January	Hilary	Barren strawberry blossom
17 January	Anthony the Abbot	Pig-nut; St Anthony's turnip (rape or bulbous crowfoot)
21 January	Agnes	Christmas rose
23 January	Conversion of Paul	Christmas rose
1 February	Bridget	St Bridget anemone; Dandelion
3 February	Blaise	Teasel; thistle
6 February	Dorothy	Apples; roses
14 February	Valentine	Crocus
22 February	Margaret of Cortona	Daisy
1 March	David	Leek
12 March	Fina	White violets
17 March	Patrick	Shamrock; St Patrick's Cabbage (London pride)
18 March	Edward, king and martyr	Crown imperial
19 March	Joseph	Oleander; campanula
23 April	George	Bluebell
29 April	Robert	Herb Robert
2 May	Athanasius	Tansy
26 May	Marianne of Jesus	Lily
11 June	Barnaby	Thistle

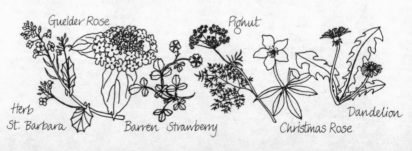

Guelder Rose   Pignut

Herb St. Barbara   Barren Strawberry   Christmas Rose   Dandelion

Date	Saint	Herb
13 June	Gerard	Herb St Gerard (goutweed)
17 June	Botolph	Turnip
24 June	John the Baptist	St John's wort; moon-daisy; great candlestick (scarlet lychnis)
25 June	James	St James' wort (ragwort)
29 June	Peter	Yellow rattle; Herb St Peter (cowslip); Samphire (from Saint Pierre)
12 July	Andrew of Rinn	Asphodel
22 July	Mary Magdalene	Costmary (maudlin-wort)
25 July	Christopher	St Christopher's herb (royal fern)
26 July	Anne	Camomile
31 July	Ignatius	St Ignatius' bean
4 August	Dominic	Rose
12 August	Clare	Lily
22 August	Philibert	Filbert
10 September	Nicholas of Tolentino	Lily
22 September	Phocas	Pink
29 September	Michael the archangel	Michaelmas daisies; Yellow archangel; angelica
6 October	Leonard	Lily of the valley
30 October	Thérèse of Lisieux	Rose
19 November	Elizabeth of Hungary	Rose
22 November	Cecilia	Roses; lilies
25 November	Catherine of Alexandria	Love-in-a-mist

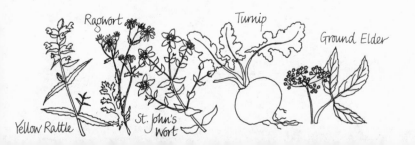

68   The flowers of the earth do no grudge at one another, though one be more beautiful and fuller of virtue than another; but they stand kindly one by another, and enjoy one another's virtue.

JAKOB BOEHME (1575–1624)

THE FLOWER GARDEN

FLOWERS IN PRAISE OF GOD

For the doubling of flowers is the improvement of the
gardeners talent.
For the flowers are great blessings.
For the Lord made a Nosegay in the meadow with his disciples
& preached upon the lily.

For the angels of God took it out of his hand and carried it
to the Height.
For a man cannot have public spirit, who is void of public
benevolence.
For there is no Height in which there are not flowers.
For flowers have great virtues for all the senses.
For the flower glorifies God and the root parries the adversary.

For the flowers have their angels even with the words of
God's Creation.
For the warp & woof of flowers are worked by perpetual
moving spirits.
For flowers are good for the living and the dead.
For there is a language of flowers.
For there is a sound reasoning upon all flowers.

For elegant phrases are nothing but flowers.
For flowers are peculiarly the poetry of Christ.
For flowers are medicinal.
For flowers are musical in ocular harmony.
For the right names of flowers are yet in heaven. God makes
gardeners better nomenclators.

CHRISTOPHER SMART (1722–1771)
Jubilate Agno

FLOWERS AND MEN

As many herbs and flowers with their fragrant sweet smells do comfort and as it were revive the spirits and perfume a whole house; even so such men as live virtuously, labouring to do good, and to profit the Church of God and the commonwealth do as it were send forth a pleasing savour of sweet instructions, not only to that time wherein they live and are fresh, but being dry, withered and dead, cease not in all after ages to do as much or more.

Many herbs and flowers that have small beauty or savour to commend them, have much more good and virtue: So many men of excellent rare parts and good qualities do lie unknown and not respected, until time and use of them do set forth their properties.

JOHN PARKINSON (1567–1650)
Paradisi in sole* Paradisus Terristris
* A pun on the words 'park-in-sun'

Thyme & Sage

THE FLOWER

How fresh, O Lord, how sweet and clean
Are thy returns! even as the flowers in spring,
   To which, besides their own demean,
The late-past frosts tributes of pleasure bring;
      Grief melts away
      Like snow in May,
As if there were no such cold thing.

Who would have thought my shrivelled heart
Could have recovered greenness? It was gone
   Quite underground; as flowers depart
To see their mother-root, when they have blown;
      Where they together
      All the hard weather,
Dead to the world, keep house unknown.

These are thy wonders, Lord of power,
Killing and quickening, bringing down to hell
   And up to heaven in an hour;
Making a chiming of a passing-bell.
      We say amiss
      This or that is;
Thy word is all, if we could spell.

O that I once past changing were,
Fast in thy Paradise, where no flower can wither!
   Many a spring I shoot up fair,
Offering at heaven, growing and groaning thither;
      Nor doth my flower
      Want a spring shower,
My sins and I joining together.

But while I grow up in a straight line,
Still upwards bent, as if heaven were mine own,
   Thy anger comes, and I decline;
What frost to that? what pole is not the zone
      Where all things burn,
      When thou dost turn,
And the least frown of thine is shown?

And now in age I bud again,
After so many deaths I live and write;
   I once more smell the dew and rain,
And relish versing. O, my only light,
       It cannot be
       That I am he
    On whom thy tempests fell all night.

These are thy wonders, Lord, of love,
To make us see we are but flowers that glide;
   Which when we once can find and prove,
Thou hast a garden for us, where to bide.
      Who would be more,
      Swelling through store,
    Forfeit their Paradise by their pride.

GEORGE HERBERT (1593–1633)

A CONTEMPLATION UPON FLOWERS

Brave flowers – that I could gallant it like you,
    And be as little vain!
You come abroad, and make a harmless show,
    And to your beds of earth again.
You are not proud: you know your birth:
For your embroider'd garments are from earth.

You do obey your months and times, but I
    Would have it ever Spring:
My fate would know no Winter, never die,
    Nor think of such a thing.
O that I could my bed of earth but view
And smile, and look as cheerfully as you!

O teach me to see Death and not to fear,
    But rather to take truce!
How often have I seen you at a bier,
    And there look fresh and spruce!
You fragrant flowers! then teach me, that my breath
Like yours may sweeten and perfume my death.

HENRY KING, BISHOP OF CHICHESTER (1592–1669)

SPRING FLOWERS

Bowing adorers of the gale,
Ye cowslips delicately pale,
  Upraise your loaded stems,
Unfold your cups in splendour; speak!
Who deck'd you with that ruddy streak,
  And gilt your golden gems?

Violets, sweet tenants of the shade,
In purple's richest pride array'd,
  Your errand here fulfil!
Go, bid the artist's simple stain
Your lustre imitate, in vain,
  And match your Maker's skill.

Daisies, ye flowers of lowly birth,
Embroid'rers of the carpet earth,
  That stud the velvet sod;
Open to spring's refreshing air,
In sweetest smiling bloom declare
  Your Maker and my God.

JOHN CLARE (1793–1850)

Cowslip Daisy & Violet

O Father, Lord!

The all-beneficent! I bless thy name,
That thou hast mantled the green earth with flowers,
Linking our hearts to nature. By the love
Of their wild blossoms, our young footsteps first
Into her deep recesses are beguiled,
Her minster cells; dark glen and forest bower,
Where, thrilling with its earliest sense of thee,
Amidst the low religious whisperings,
The shivery leaf sounds of the solitude,
The spirit wakes to worship, and is made
Thy living temple. By the breath of flowers,
Thou callest us, from city throngs and cares,
Back to the woods, the birds, the mountain streams,
That sing of thee! back to free childhood's heart,
Fresh with the dews of tenderness! – thou bidd'st
The lilies of the field with placid smile
Reprove man's feverish strivings, and infuse
Through his worn soul a more unworldly life,
With their soft holy breath. Thou hast not left
His purer nature, with its fine desires,
Uncared for in this universe of thine.
The glowing rose attests it, the beloved
Of poet hearts, touched by their fervent dreams
With spiritual light, and made a source
Of heaven-ascending thoughts. E'en to faint age
Thou lend'st the vernal bliss: – the old man's eye
Falls on the kindling blossoms, and his soul
Remembers youth and love, and hopefully
Turns unto thee, who call'st earth's buried germs
From dust to splendour; as the mortal seed
Shall, at thy summons, from the grave spring up
To put on glory, to be girt with power,
And filled with immortality. Receive
Thanks, blessings, love, for these, thy lavish boons,
And, most of all, their heavenward influences,
O thou that gav'st us flowers.

FELICIA HEMANS (1793–1835)

LIFE

I made a posie while the day ran by:
Here will I smell my remnant out, and tie
        My life within this band;
But Time did becken to the flow'rs, and they
By noon most cunningly did steal away,
        And wither'd in my hand.

My hand was next to them, and then my heart;
I took, without more thinking, in good part
        Time's gentle admonition;
Who did so sweetly Death's sad taste convey,
Making my minde to smell my fatall day,
        Yet sugring the suspicion.

Farewell, deare flow'rs; sweetly your time ye spent,
Fit while ye lived for smell or ornament,
        And after death for cures.
I follow straight, without complaints or grief;
Since if my scent be good, I care not if
        It be as short as yours.

GEORGE HERBERT (1593–1633)

HYMN FOR THE FEAST OF ST PHILIP
AND ST JAMES

Now the winds are all composure,
    But the breath upon the bloom,
Blowing sweet o'er each inclosure,
    Grateful off'rings of perfume.

Tansy, calaminth and daisies,
    On the river's margin thrive;
And accompany the mazes
    Of the stream that leaps alive.

Muse, accordant to the season,
    Give the numbers life and air;
When the sounds and objects reason
    In behalf of praise and pray'r.

All the scenes of nature quicken,
    By the genial spirit fann'd;
And the painted beauties thicken
    Colour'd by the master's hand.

Earth her vigour repossessing
    As the blasts are held in ward;
Blessing heap'd and press'd on blessing,
    Yield the measure of the Lord.

Beeches, without order seemly,
    Shade the flow'rs of annual birth,
And the lily smiles supremely
    Mentioned by the Lord on earth.

Cowslips seize upon the fallow,
    And the cardamine in white,
Where the corn-flow'rs join the mallow,
    Joy in health, and thrift unite.

Study sits beneath her arbour,
    By the bason's glossy side;
While the boat from out its harbour
    Exercise and pleasure guide.

Pray'r and praise be mine employment,
    Without grudging or regret;
Lasting life, and long enjoyment,
    Are not here, and are not yet.

Hark! aloud, the black-bird whistles,
    With surrounding fragrance blest,
And the goldfinch in the thistles
    Makes provision for her nest.

Tansy

Calamint

Daisy

Ev'n the hornet hives his honey,
     Bluecap builds his stately dome,
And the rocks supply the coney
     With a fortress and an home.

But the servants of their Saviour,
     Which with gospel peace are shod,
Have no bed but what the paviour
     Makes them in the porch of God.

O thou house that hold'st the charter
     Of salvation from on high,
Fraught with prophet, saint, and martyr,
     Born to weep, to starve and die!

Great today thy song and rapture
     In the choir of Christ and WREN
When two prizes were the capture
     Of the hand that fish'd for men.

To the man of quick compliance
     Jesus call'd, and Philip came;
And began to make alliance
     For his master's cause and name.

James, of title most illustrious,
     Brother of the Lord, allow'd;
In the vineyard how industrious,
     Nor by years nor hardship bow'd!

Each accepted in his trial,
     One the CHEERFUL one the JUST:
Both of love and self-denial,
     Both of everlasting trust.

Living they dispens'd salvation,
     Heav'n-endow'd with grace and pow'r;
And they dy'd in imitation
     Of their Saviour's final hour.

Who, for cruel traitors pleading,
     Triumph'd in his parting breath;
O'er all miracles preceding
     His inestimable death.

Beech

Lily

Cowslip

Lady's Smock

Mallow

Cornflower

CHRISTOPHER SMART (1722–1771)

EMPLOYMENT I

If, as a flowre doth spread and die,
    Thou wouldst extend to me to some good,
Before I were by frost's extremitie
        Nipt in the bud;

The sweetnesse and the praise were Thine,
    But the extension and the room
Which in Thy garland I should fill were mine
        At Thy great doom.

For as Thou dost impart Thy grace,
    The greater shall our glorie be;
The measure of our joyes is in this place,
        The stuffe with Thee.

Let me not languish, then, and spend
    A life as barren to Thy praise
As is the dust to which that life doth tend,
        But with delaies.

All things are busie; onely I
    Neither bring hony with the bees,
Nor flowres to make that, nor the husbandrie
        To water these.

I am no link of Thy great chain,
    But all my companie is a weed.
Lord, place me in Thy consort; give one strain
        To my poore reed.

GEORGE HERBERT (1593–1633)

A BLESSING OF HERBS AND FLOWERS

Almighty, everlasting God, by thy Word alone thou hast made
heaven, earth, sea, all things visible and invisible, and hast adorned
the earth with plants and trees for the use of men and animals.
Thou appointest each species to bring forth fruit in its kind, not
only to serve as food for living creatures, but also as medicine to sick
bodies. With mind and word we earnestly appeal to thine ineffable
goodness to bless these various herbs and fruits, and add to their
natural powers the grace of thy new blessing. May they ward off
disease and adversity from men and beasts who use them in thy
name. Through our Lord, Jesus Christ, Thy Son, Who liveth and
reigneth with thee in unity of the Holy Spirit, God, forever and
ever. Amen.

Ritual

Snowdrop

Crocus

Daffodil

Lily

Poppy

Rose

Camomile

Sunflower

The Snowdrop in purest white array
First rears her head on Candlemas day;
While the crocus hastens to the shrine
Of Primrose lone on St Valentine.
Then comes the Daffodil beside
Our Lady's Smock at our Lady-tide.
About St George, when blue is worn,
The blue Harebells the fields adorn;
Against the day of Holy Cross,
The Crowfoot gilds the flowery grass.
When St Barnaby bright smiles night and day,
Poor Ragged Robin blossoms in the hay.
The Scarlet Lychnis, the garden's pride,
Flames at St John the Baptist's tide.
From Visitation to St Swithin's showers,
The Lily white reigns Queen of the flowers;
And Poppies a sanguine mantle spread
For the blood of the Dragon St Margaret shed.
Then under the wanton Rose, again,
That blushes for Penitent Magdalen,
Till Lammas day, called August's Wheel,
When the long corn stinks of Camomile.
When Mary left us here below,
The Virgin's Bower is full in blow,
And yet anon, the full Sunflower blew,
And became a star for Bartholomew.
The Passion-flower long has blowed,
To betoken us signs of Holy Rood.
The Michaelmas Daisies, among dead weeds,
Blooms for St Michael's valourous deeds;
And seems the last of flowers that stood,
Till the feast of St Simon and St Jude –
Save Mushrooms, and the Fungus race,
That grow till All-Hallow-tide takes place.
Soon the evergreen Laurel alone is green,
When Catherine crowns all learned men.
The Ivy and Holly berries are seen,
And Yule Log and Wassails come round again.

ANONYMOUS

Parasol Mushroom

A NOSEGAY

84

I read in an old Monkish written Herbal, wherein the Author writeth, that this herb did signify the Holy Trinity: and therefore was called the Herb of the Trinity, and thus he made his allegory. This flower is but one in which, said he, are three sundry colours, and yet but one sweet savour. So God is three distinct persons, in one Undivided Trinity, united in one eternal glory, and divine Majesty.

God send thee heart's-ease. For it is much better with poverty to have the same, than to be a king, with a miserable mind. For, from thence springeth either felicity, or adversity: an image of heaven with joy, or else with inward horror of mind, and vexation . . . pray God give thee but one handful of heavenly heart's-ease, which passeth all the pleasant flowers that grow in this world.

WILLIAM BULLEIN
Herbal (1562)

THE PASSION FLOWER

The Passion Flower (*Passiflora coerulaea*) was discovered by Jesuits
when they first ventured on their missions to Peru in the seventeeth
century. It lent itself perfectly as a visual aid to the Passion narrative
in the following way:

> The hand-shaped leaves are the hands of Christ's persecutors.
> The tendrils are the ropes that bound Him, and the whips that
> scourged Him.
> The pistil is the column to which Christ was tied to be
> scourged.
> The five sepals and five petals are the ten disciples, excluding
> Peter who denied Him, and Judas who betrayed Him.
> The five stamens represent the five wounds and
> The triple style looks like the three nails.
> The seed-pod represents the sponge dipped in vinegar held up
> for Christ to drink.
> The filaments look like the crown of thorns.
> The corona represents the nimbus which surrounded Christ's
> head.

The flower blooms for about three days, which, of course, was the
time between the Passion and the Resurrection. And it is blue – the
colour of Heaven.

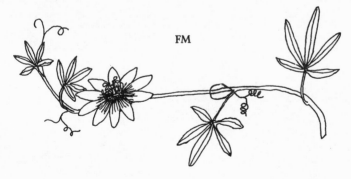

FM

THE AMARANTH

                To the ground
With solemn adoration down they cast
Their crowns inwove with Amarant and gold,
Immortal Amarant, a flower which once
In Paradise, fast by the tree of life,
Began to bloom; but soon for man's offence
To heaven removed, where first it grew, there grows,
And flowers aloft, shading the fount of life,
And where the river of bliss through midst of Heaven
Rolls o'er Elysian flowers her amber stream;
With these, that never fade, the spirits elect
Bind their resplendent locks enwreathed with beams,
Now in loose garlands thick thrown off; the bright
Pavement, that like a sea of jasper shone,
Empurpled with celestial roses, smiled.

JOHN MILTON (1608–1674)

DIALOGUE OF THE FLOWERS

The Heliotrope . . .   Through all the changes of the day
           I turn me to the sun;
           In clear or cloudy skies I say
           Alike – Thy will be done!

The Violet . . .   A lowly flower, in secret bower,
           Invisible I dwell;
           For blessing made, without parade,
           Known only by the smell.

The Lily . . .   Emblem of Him, in whom no stain
           The eye of heaven could see,
           In all their glory, monarchs vain
           Are not array'd like me.

The Rose . . .   With ravish'd heart that crimson hail,
           Which in my bosom glows:
           Think how the lily of the vale
           Became like Sharon's rose.

The Primrose . . .   When time's dark winter shall be o'er,
           His storms and tempests laid;
           Like me you'll rise, a fragrant flower.
           But not like me to fade.

The Garden . . .   The bower of innocence and bliss,
           Sin caused to disappear;
           Repent, and walk in faith and love –
           You'll find an Eden here.

GEORGE HORNE (1730–1792)

THE SUNFLOWER

Eagle of flowers! I see thee stand,
    And on the sun's noon-glory gaze:
With eye like his thy lids expand,
    And fringe their disk with golden rays;
Though fix'd on earth, in darkness rooted there,
Light is thine element, thy dwelling air,
      Thy prospect heaven.

So would mine eagle-soul descry,
    Beyond the path where planets run,
The light of immortality,
    The splendour of creation's sun;
Though sprung from earth, and hast'ning to the tomb,
In hope a flower or paradise to bloom,
      I look to heaven.

JAMES MONTGOMERY (1771–1854)

ULEX

Ulex! that dost crown with gold
All the wild and breezy heath,
Forming many a gorgeous wreath
Fragrant with thy odorous breath,
Be my emblem – bright and bold,
Happy in an humble station,
Lending smiles to desolation;
Blooming gaily, though so lowly,
Raising aspirations holy;
Thorny spines surrounding thee,
Yet kindly sheltering bird and bee;
Lustre and joy diffusing round
O'er the rough and desert ground;
Firm and useful, cheerful, free, –
Let me then resemble thee.

ANONYMOUS
From a Victorian book, *The Language of Flowers*

THE LILY

How wither'd, perish'd, seems the form
    Of yon obscure unsightly root!
Yet from the blight of wintry storm
    It hides secure the precious fruit.

The careless eye can find no grace,
    No beauty in the scaly folds,
Nor see within the dark embrace
    What latent loveliness it holds.

Yet in that bulb, those sapless scales
    The lily wraps her silver vest,
Till vernal suns and vernal gales
    Shall kiss once more her fragrant breast.

Yes, hide beneath the mould'ring heap,
    The undelighting slighted thing;
There in the cold earth buried deep,
    In the silence let it wait the spring.

Oh! many a stormy night shall close
    In gloom upon the barren earth,
While still in undisturb'd repose,
    Uninjured lies the future birth.

And ignorance, with sceptic eye,
    Hope's patient smile shall wond'ring view;
Or mock her fond credulity,
    As her soft tears the spot bedew.

Sweet smile of hope, delicious tear,
    The sun, the show'r indeed shall come
The promis'd verdant shoot appear,
    And nature bid her blossoms bloom.

And thou, O virgin queen of spring,
      Shalt from thy dark and lowly bed,
Bursting thy green sheath's silken string,
      Unveil thy charms, and perfume shed.

Unfold thy robes of purest white,
      Unsullied from their darksome grave,
And thy soft petal's flow'ry light,
      In the mild breeze unfetter'd wave.

So faith shall seek the lowly dust,
      Where humble sorrow loves to lie,
And bid her thus her hopes intrust,
      And watch with patient, cheerful eye;

And bear the long, cold, wintry night,
      And bear her own degraded doom,
And wait till heav'n reviving light,
      Eternal spring! shall burst the gloom.

MARY TIGHE (1773–1810)

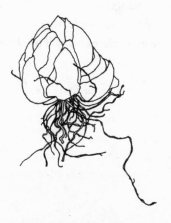

TO THE FLOWER, FORGET-ME-NOT

'I muse on the works of thy hands.' Psalm 143:5

Thou sweet little flower with the bright blue eye,
That peepest from the bank so modestly,
Thou art come from a source invisible,
And thou hast some important words to tell.

Thou art come like the 'still small voice' of Him,
Who whispers his truth in the evening dim;
Who shines in the stars in the azure sky,
And gems the dark world with piety.

Thou art come as a warning to wandering souls,
Who are careless of time, as it swiftly rolls;
And forgetful of God, who upholds their lot,
But who whispers in thee – forget me not.

Thou art come as a gift from a friend sincere,
Whose dwelling is fixed in the heavenly sphere,
But whose spirit is with us in every spot,
And the voice of those works is – forget me not.

Thou art come to repeat an assurance of love,
From that changeless friend in the mansions above:
To the soul that loves Christ in sincerity,
His goodness declares – I will not forget thee.

Gems of Sacred Poetry (19th century)

THE DAISY

Not worlds on worlds in phalanx deep,
    Need we to prove a God is here;
The daisy, fresh from winter sleek,
    Tells of His hand in lines as clear.

For who but He who arched the skies,
    And pours the day-spring's living flood,
Wondrous alike in all He tries,
    Could rear the daisy's purple bud?

Mould its green cup, its wiry stem;
    Its fringed border nicely spin;
And cut the gold embossed gem,
    That, set in silver, gleams within?

And fling it, unrestrained and free,
    O'er hill and dale, and desert sod,
That man where'er he walks may see,
    In every step, the stamp of God.

JOHN MASON GOOD (19th century)

TO A DAISY

Slight as thou art, thou art enough to hide,
    Like all created things, secrets from me,
    And stand a barrier to eternity.
And I, how can I praise thee well and wide

From where I dwell – upon the hither side?
    Thou little veil for so great mystery,
    When shall I penetrate all things and thee,
And then look back? For this I must abide,

Till thou shalt grow and fold and be unfurled
Literally between me and the world.
    Then I shall drink from in beneath a spring,

And from a poet's side shall read his book.
O daisy mine, what will it be to look
    From God's side even of such a simple thing?

ALICE MEYNELL (1847–1922)

FLOWER IN THE CRANNIED WALL

Flower in the crannied wall,
I pluck you out of the crannies; –
Hold you here, root and all, in my hand,
Little flower – but if I could understand
What you are, root and all, and all in all,
I should know what God and man is.

ALFRED, LORD TENNYSON (1809–1890)

DAISIES ARE OUR SILVER

Daisies are our silver,
      Buttercups our gold:
This is all the treasure
      We can have or hold.

Raindrops are our diamonds
      And the morning dew;
While for shining sapphires
      We've the speedwell blue.

These shall be our emeralds –
      Leaves so new and green;
Roses make the reddest
      Rubies ever seen.

God, who gave these treasures
      To your children small
Teach us how to love them
      And grow like them all.

Make us bright as silver:
      Make us good as gold;
Warm as summer roses
      Let our hearts unfold.

Gay as leaves in April,
      Clear as drops of dew –
God, who made the speedwell,
      Keep us true to you.

JAN STRUTHER

MORNING GLORY

With a pure colour there is little one can do:
Of a pure thing there is little one can say.
We are dumb in the face of that cold blush of blue,
Called glory, and enigmatic as the face of day.

A couple of optical tricks are there for the mind;
See how the azure darkens as we recede:
Like the delectable mountains left behind,
Region and colour too absolute for our need.

Or putting an eye too close, until it blurs,
You see a firmament, a ring of sky,
With a white radiance in it, a universe,
And something there that might seem to sing and fly.

Only the double sex, the usual thing;
But it calls to mind spirit, it seems like one
Who hovers in brightness suspended and shimmering,
Crying Holy and hanging in the eye of the sun.

And there is one thing more; as in despair
The eye dwells on that ribbed pentagonal round,
A cold sidereal whisper brushes the ear,
A prescient tingling, a prophecy of sound.

RUTH PITTER (b. 1897)

THE ROSE GARDEN

HOW ROSES FIRST CAME INTO THE WORLD

From Hebron men go to Bethlehem in half a day, for it is but five miles; and it is full fair way, by plains and woods full delectable. Bethlehem is a little city, long and narrow and well walled, and in each side enclosed with good ditches; and it was wont to be clept Ephrata, as holy writ saith, Ecce, audivimus eum in Ephrata, that is to say, 'Lo, we heard him in Ephrata.' And toward the east end of the city is a full fair church and a gracious, and it hath many towers, pinnacles and corners, full strong and curiously made; and within that church be forty-four pillars of marble, great and fair.

And between the city and the church is the field Floridus, that is to say, the 'field flourished'. For as much as a fair maiden was blamed with wrong, and slandered that she had done fornication; for which cause she was demned to death, and to be burnt in that place, to the which she was led. And, as the fire began to burn about here, she made her prayers to our Lord, that as wisely as she was not guilty of that sin, that he would help her and make it to be known to all men, of his merciful grace. And when she had thus said, she entered into the fire, and anon was the fire quenched and out; and the brands that were burning became red rose-trees, and the brands that were not kindled became white rose-trees and roses, both white and red, that ever any man saw; and thus was this maiden saved by the grace of God. And therefore is that field clept the field of God flourished, for it was full of roses.

SIR JOHN MANDEVILLE (14th century)
The Voyages and Travels of Sir John Mandeville, Kt

THE ROSE

Before man's fall, the rose was born,
S. Ambrose says, without the thorn:
But, for man's fault, then was the thorn,
Without the fragrant rose-bud, born;
But ne'er the rose without the thorn.

ROBERT HERRICK (1591–1674)

100

Lat no man booste of conning nor vertu,
Of tresour, richesse, nor of sapience,
Of wordly support, for all cometh of Jesu:
Counsail, comfort, discrecioun and prudence,
Provisioun, forsight, and providence,
Like as the Lord of grace list dispoose;
Som man hath wisdom, som man hath elloquence –
All stant on chaung, like a midsomer roose.

Wholsom in smelling be the soote floures,
Full delitable, outward, to the sight;
The thorn is sharp, curyd with fresh coloures;   (covered)
All is nat gold that outward sheweth bright;
A stokfish boon in dirkeness yeveth a light,
Twen fair and foul, as God list dispoose,
A difference atwix day and night –
All stant on chaunge like a midsomer roose.

It was the Roose of the bloody feeld,
Roose of Jericho that grew in Beedlem   (Bethlehem)
The five rooses portrayed in the sheeld,
Splayed in the baneer at Jerusalem:
The sonne was clips, and dirk in every rem,   (eclipsed, realm)
Whan Christ Jesu five welles list uncloose
Toward Paradis, called the rede strem –
Of whos five woundes prent in your hert a roose.

JOHN LYDGATE (?1370–?1451)

SEE THE VIRGIN ROSE

Ah! see, who so fair thing dost fain to see,
In springing flower the image of thy day!
Ah! see the virgin rose, how sweetly she
Doth first peep forth with bashful modesty,
That fairer seems, the less ye see her may!
Lo! see soon after, how more bold and free
Her barèd bosom she doth broad display!
Lo! see soon after, how she fades and falls away!

So passeth, in the passing of a day,
Of mortal life, the leaf, the bud, the flower.

EDMUND SPENSER (1552–1599)

OF A ROSE, A LOVELY ROSE,
OF A ROSE IS AL MYN SONG

Lestenyt, lordynges, both elde and yinge,
How this rose began to sprynge;
Swych a rose to myn lykynge
     In al this word ne knowe I non.

The aungil came fro hevene tour
To grete Marye with gret honour,
And seyde sche xuld bere the flour
     That xulde breke the fyndes bond.

The flour sprong in heye Bedlem,
That is bothe bryht and schen:
The rose is Mary, hevene qwen,
     Out of here bosum the blosme sprong.

The ferste braunche is ful of myht,
The sprong on Cyrstemesse nyht,
The sterre schon over Bedlem bryt
    That is bothe brod and long.

The secunde braunche sprong to helle,
The fendys power doun to felle:
Therein myht non sowle dwelle;
    Blyssid be the time the rose sprong!

The thredde braunche is good and swote,   (sweet)
It sprange to hevene, crop and rote,
Therein to dwellyn and ben our bote;   (salvation)
    Every day it schewit in prystes hond.

Prey we to here with gret honour,
She that bar the blyssid flowr,
She be our helpe and our socour
    And schyld us fro the fyndes bond.

ANONYMOUS (c. 1400)

THE ROSE

Presse me not to take more pleasure
    In this world of sugred lies,
And to use a larger measure
    Then my strict, yet welcome size.

First, there is no pleasure here:
    Colour'd griefs indeed there are,
Blushing woes, that look as cleare
    As if they could beautie spare.

Or if such deceits there be,
    Such delights I meant to say;
There are no such things to me,
    Who have pass'd my right away.

But I will not much oppose
    Unto what you now advise:
Onely take this gentle rose,
    And therein my answer lies.

What is fairer then a rose?
    What is sweeter? yet it purgeth
Purgings enmitie disclose,
    Enmitie forbearance urgeth.

If then all that worldlings prize
    Be contracted to a rose;
Sweetly there indeed it lies,
    But it biteth in the close.

So this flower doth judge and sentence
    Worldly joyes to be a scourge:
For they all produce repentance,
    And repentance is a purge.

But I health, not physick choose:
    Onely though I you oppose,
Say that fairly I refuse,
    For my answer is a rose.

GEORGE HERBERT (1593–1633)

THERE IS NO ROSE

There is no rose of such vertu
As is the rose that bare Jesu.
            Alleluia.

For in this rose containèd was
Heaven and earth in little space:
            Res miranda.

By that rose we may well see
There be one God in persons three:
            Pares forma.

The angels sungen, the shepherds too:
Gloria in excelsis Deo:
            Gaudeamus.

Leave we all this wordly mirth,
And follow we this joyful birth:
            Transeamus.

ANONYMOUS (15th century)

ES IST EIN' ROS' ENTSPRUNGEN

There is a flower springing
    From tender roots it grows,
From Eden beauty bringing
    From Jesse's stem a rose,
    On his green branch it blows:
A bud that in cold winter
    At midnight will unclose.

Pure Mary, maiden holy,
    The dream by prophets seen,
Who in a stable lowly
    Above her child did lean
    So gentle and serene:
This was Esaias' vision,
    The tree of living green.

To Mary, rose of heaven,
    With loving hearts we say
Let our sins be forgiven,
    And grief be turned away
    Upon this Christmas Day:
To Jesus, child of winter,
    For grace and hope we pray.

German carol
Translated by Ursula Vaughan Williams

VIRTUE

Sweet day, so cool, so calm, so bright!
The bridal of the earth and sky –
The dew shall weep thy fall to-night;
            For thou must die.

Sweet rose, whose hue angry and brave
Bids the rash gazer wipe his eye,
Thy root is ever in its grave,
            And thou must die.

Sweet spring, full of sweet days and roses,
A box where sweets compacted lie,
My music shows ye have your closes,
            And all must die.

Only a sweet and virtuous soul,
Like season'd timber, never gives;
But though the whole world turn to coal,
            Then chiefly lives.

GEORGE HERBERT (1593–1633)

WELCOME, GOLDEN ROSE!

When the herds were watching
    In the midnight chill,
Came a spotless lambkin
    From the heavenly hill.

Snow was on the mountains
    And the wind was cold,
When from God's own garden
    Dropped a rose of gold.

When 'twas bitter winter,
    Homeless and forlorn
In a star-lit stable
    Christ the babe was born.

Welcome, heavenly lambkin;
    Welcome, golden rose;
Alleluya, baby
    In the swaddling clothes!

WILLIAM CANTON (1845–1926)

THE MYSTERY

He came and took me by the hand
    Up to a red rose tree,
He kept His meaning to Himself
    But gave a rose to me.

I did not pray Him to lay bare
    The mystery to me,
Enough the rose was Heaven to smell,
    And His own face to see.

RALPH HODGSON (1871–1962)

THE CROWN OF ROSES

When Jesus Christ was yet a child
He had a garden small and wild,
Wherein he cherished roses fair,
And wove them into garlands there.

Now once, as summer time drew nigh,
There came a troop of children by,
And seeing roses on the tree,
With shouts they plucked them merrily.

'Do you bind roses in your hair?'
They cried, in scorn, to Jesus there.
The boy said humbly: 'Take, I pray,
All but the naked thorns away.'

Then of the thorns they made a crown,
And with rough fingers pressed it down,
Till on his forehead fair and young
Red drops of blood like roses sprung.

PLECHTCHÉEV

THE HOT HOUSE

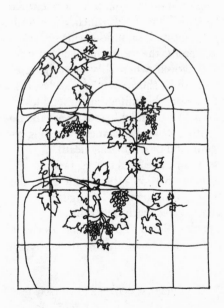

WHO LOVES A GARDEN

Who loves a garden, loves a greenhouse too.
Unconscious of a less propitious clime,
There blooms exotic beauty, warm and snug,
While the winds whistle and the snows descend.
The spiry myrtle with unwithering leaf
Shines there and flourishes. The golden boast
Of Portugal and western India there,
The ruddier orange and the paler lime,
Peep through their polish'd foliage at the storm
And seem to smile at what they need not fear.
The amomum there with intermingling flowers
And cherries hangs her twigs. Geranium boasts
Her crimson honours, and the spangled beau,
Ficoides, glitters bright the winter long.
All plants, of every leaf that can endure
The winter's frown, if screened from his shrewd bite
Live there and prosper . . .
                    . . . Much yet remains
Unsung, and many cares are yet behind,
And more laborious; cares on which depends
Their vigour, injured soon, not soon restored.
The soil must be renew'd, which, often wash'd,
Loses its treasure of salubrious salts,
And disappoints the roots; the slender roots
Close interwoven, where they meet the vase
Must smooth be shorn away; the sapless branch
Must fly before the knife; the wither'd leaf
Must be detach'd, and where it strews the floor
Swept with a woman's neatness, breeding else
Contagion, and disseminating death.
Discharge but these kind offices, (and who
Would spare, that loves them, offices like these?)
Well they reward the toil. The sight is pleased,
The scent regaled, each odiferous leaf,
Each opening blossom, freely breathes abroad
Its gratitude, and thanks him with its sweets.

WILLIAM COWPER (1731–1800)
The Task – The Garden

The trees of the Lord are full of sap;
The cedars of Lebanon, which he hath planted;
Where the birds make their nests:
As for the stork, the fir trees are her house.

Psalm 104:16–18

114   And Solomon sent to Hiram, saying . . .

. . . And, behold, I purpose to build an house unto the name
of the Lord my God, as the Lord spake unto David my father,
saying, Thy son, whom I will set upon thy throne in thy room, he
shall build an house unto my name. Now therefore command thou
that they hew me cedar trees out of Lebanon; and my servants shall
be with thy servants: and unto thee will I give hire for thy servants
according to all that thou shalt appoint: for thou knowest that there
is not among us any that can skill to hew timber like unto the
Sidonians.

And it came to pass, when Hiram heard the words of
Solomon, that he rejoiced greatly, and said, Blessed be the Lord this
day, which hath given unto David a wise son over this great people.
And Hiram sent to Solomon, saying, I have considered the things
which thou sentest to me for: and I will do all thy desire concerning
timber of cedar, and concerning timber of fir. My servants shall
bring them down from Lebanon unto the sea: and I will convey
them by sea in floats unto the place that thou shalt appoint me, and
will cause them to be discharged there, and thou shalt receive them:
and thou shalt accomplish my desire, in giving food for my
household. So Hiram gave Solomon cedar trees and fir trees
according to all his desire . . .

1 Kings 5:5–10

SOLOMON'S WISDOM

And Solomon's wisdom excelled the wisdom of all the children of
the east country, and all the wisdom of Egypt. For he was wiser
than all men; than Ethan the Ezrahite, and Heman, and Chalcol,
and Darda, the sons of Mahol: and his fame was in all nations round
about. And he spake three thousand proverbs: and his songs were a
thousand and five. And he spake of trees, from the cedar tree that is
in Lebanon even unto the hyssop that springeth out of the wall . . .

1 Kings 4:30–32

116   The trees went forth on a time to anoint a king over them; and they said unto the olive tree, Reign thou over us. But the olive tree said unto them, Should I leave my fatness, wherewith by me they honour God and man, and go to be promoted over the trees? And the trees said to the fig tree, Come thou and reign over us. But the fig tree said unto them, Should I forsake my sweetness, and my good fruit, and go to be promoted over the trees? Then said the trees unto the vine, Come thou, and reign over us. And the vine said unto them, Should I leave my wine, which cheereth God and man, and go to be promoted over the trees? Then said all the trees unto the bramble, Come thou, and reign over us. And the bramble said unto the trees, If in truth ye anoint me king over you, then come and put your trust in my shadow: and if not, let fire come out of the bramble, and devour the cedars of Lebanon . . .

Judges 9:8–15

EZEKIEL'S PARABLE OF THE CEDAR

Thus saith the Lord God; I will also take off the highest branch of the high cedar, and will set it; I will crop off from the top of his young twigs a tender one, and will plant it upon an high mountain and eminent: in the mountain of the height of Israel will I plant it: and it shall bring forth boughs, and bear fruit, and be a goodly cedar: and under it shall dwell all fowl of every wing; in the shadow of the branches thereof shall they dwell. And all the trees of the field shall know that I the Lord have brought down the high tree, have exalted the low tree, have dried up the green tree, and have made the dry tree to flourish: I the Lord have spoken and have done it.

Ezekiel 17:22–24

THE BANIAN TREE, OR INDIAN FIG

The banian-tree, or Indian fig, is a native of several parts of the East Indies. It has a wooden stem, branching to a great height and vast extent, with heart-shaped entire leaves ending in acute points. This tree is beautifully described by Milton:

> There soon they chose
> The fig-tree: not that kind for fruit renown'd;
> But such as, at this day to Indians known
> In Malabar or Decan, spreads her arms,
> Branching so broad and long, that in the ground
> The bending twigs take root, and daughters grow
> About the mother-tree, a pillar'd shade
> High over-arch'd, and echoing walks between.
> There oft the Indian herdsman, shunning heat,
> Shelters in cool, and tends his pasturing herds
> At loop-holes cut through thickest shade.

Paradise Lost, Book 9, lines 1100–1110

Indeed, the banian-tree is the most beautiful of Nature's productions in that genial climate, where she sports with so much profusion and variety. Some of these trees are of amazing size and great extent, as they are continually increasing, and contrary to most other things in animal and vegetable life, seem to be exempt from decay. Every branch from the main body throws out its roots; at first in small tender fibres, several yards from the ground: these continually grow thicker until they reach the surface; and there striking in, they increase to large trunks, and become parent trees, shooting out new branches from the top: these in time suspend their roots, which swelling into trunks, produce other branches; thus continuing in a state of progression as long as the earth, the first parent of them all, contributes her sustenance. The Hindoos are peculiarly fond of the banian-tree. They look upon it as an emblem of the Deity; from its long duration, its out-stretching arms, and over-shadowing beneficence. They almost pay it divine honours. Near these trees the most esteemed pagodas are generally erected: under their shade the Brahmins spend their lives in religious solitude: and the natives of all casts and tribes are fond of recreating in the cool recesses, beautiful walks, and lovely vistas, of this umbrageous canopy, impervious to the hottest beams of a tropical sun . . . This tree not only affords shelter, but sustenance to all its inhabitants; being covered amidst its bright foliage with small figs of a rich scarlet, on which they all regale with as much delight as the lords of the creation on their more various and costly fare.

The Class Book: or, Three hundred and Sixty-five Reading Lessons, Adapted to the Use of Schools; for Every Day in the Year, Selected, Arranged, and Compiled, from the Best Authors, by the Rev. David Blair (1823)

The Perindeus is a tree in India. Its fruit is very sweet and exceedingly agreeable. Doves delight in the produce of this tree, and live in it, feeding on its fruits.

Now the dragon is an enemy to doves, but it fears the tree they live in, and its shade too, nor can it approach either the tree or its shadow. Indeed, if the shadow of the tree falls to the west, the dragon betakes himself to the east, and if the shadow comes to the east, he flees to the west. If, however, a dove happens to be found outside the tree-shade then the dragon kills it.

Understand that the tree is God the Father and the shade is God the Son, for Gabriel said to Mary: 'The Holy Ghost shall come upon thee, and the shade of the all-highest shall overshadow thee'. The fruit of the tree is heavenly wisdom, i.e. of the Lord. The dove is the Holy Ghost.

Look to it, therefore, O Man, lest before you can receive the Holy Ghost, which is the spiritual and heavenly dove descending and abiding in you, you do not remain for eternity outside the Father, Son and Holy Ghost. Look to it lest the Dragon destroy you, i.e. the Devil.

Now if you have the Holy Ghost, the Dragon cannot come nigh you. O Man, then turn toward the Catholic faith and remain in it and there live. Persevere there in the one Catholic Church. Take as much care lest that Dragon, the serpent of old, should seize you and gobble you up like Judas – who, as soon as he went out from the Lord and his brother apostles, was instantly devoured by a demon and perished.

The Book of Beasts, a translation by T.H. White (1906–1964) from a twelfth-century Latin bestiary.

I AM THE TRUE VINE

I am the true vine, and my Father is the husbandman. Every branch in me that beareth not fruit he taketh away: and every branch that beareth fruit, he purgeth it, that it may bring forth more. Now ye are clean through the word which I have spoken unto you. Abide in me, and I in you. As the branch cannot bear fruit of itself, except it abide in the vine; no more can ye, except ye abide in me. I am the vine, ye are the branches: He that abideth in me, and I in him, the same bringeth forth much fruit: for without me ye can do nothing. If a man abide not in me, he is cast forth as a branch, and is withered; and men gather them, and cast them into the fire, and they are burned . . . Ye have not chosen me, but I have chosen you, and ordained you, that ye should go and bring forth fruit, and that your fruit should remain: that whatsoever ye shall ask of the Father in my name, he may give it you.

John 15:1–6, 16

122

Most blessèd Vine!
Whose juice so good
I feel as wine,
But thy fair branches felt as blood;
How wert thou pressed
To be my feast!
In what deep anguish
Didst thou languish,
What springs of sweat and blood did drown thee!
How in one path
Did the full wrath
Of thy great Father
Crowd and gather,
Doubling thy griefs, when none would own thee!

HENRY VAUGHAN (1622–1695)

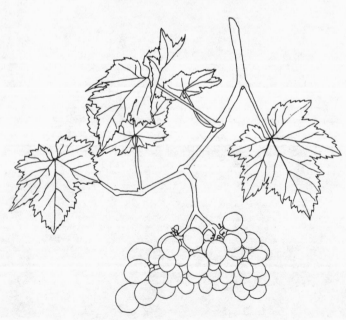

THE VINE

The wine of Love is music,
     And the feast of Love is song;
And when Love sits down to the banquet,
     Love sits long:

Sits long and arises drunken,
     But not with the feast and the wine;
He reeleth with his own heart,
     That great, rich Vine.

JAMES THOMSON (1834–1882)

124   . . . and if the root be holy, so are the branches. And if some of the branches be broken off, and thou, being a wild olive tree, wert graffed in among them, and with them partakest of the root and fatness of the olive tree; boast not against the branches. But if thou boast, thou bearest not the root, but the root thee.

Thou wilt say then, the branches were broken off, that I might be graffed in.

Well; because of unbelief they were broken off, and thou standest by faith. Be not highminded, but fear: for if God spared not the natural branches, take heed lest he also spare not thee. Behold therefore the goodness and severity of God: on them which fell, severity; but toward thee, goodness, if thou continue in his goodness: otherwise thou also shalt be cut off. And they also, if they abide not still in unbelief, shall be graffed in: for God is able to graff them in again. For if thou wert cut out of the olive tree which is wild by nature, and wert graffed contrary to nature into a good olive tree: how much more shall these, which be the natural branches, be graffed into their own olive tree?

Romans 11:16–24

OLIVE TREES

God must have had fun creating olive trees.
To have thought of and made a tree of any kind needed the supreme
    Creator,
but then to have decided to make one
so individual
so unique
and to have placed it exquisitely
against the Mediterranean blue!

I see them leading the way down the steep incline to the rocky shore,
defying description;
trunks twisted and gnarled beyond mere Man's imagining;
shapes to haunt dreams,
producing their wealth of grey-green silvery leaves
and fruits unlike all others.

I think that God is still amused about the olive trees,
and that his laughter plays amongst their leaves
setting them dancing.

MARGARET ORFORD

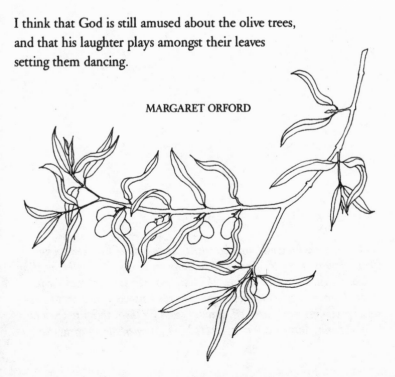

THE FIG TREE CURSED

Like as the braving green, but barren, tree
(That flourished fair when not a fig was found)
Christ cursed with, 'Never fruit grow more on thee',
Because it did no good, but cumber ground:
>So fares the false deluding show of mine,
>Green-leaved beginning, withered fruitless fine.

SAMUEL ROWLANDS (?1570–?1630)

I have included these pieces because I am so fond of figs even though Christ's words about the fig tree are usually troubling. Especially puzzling was his cursing of the fig tree. William Barclay explains that the fig would not be expected to produce fruit in the Passover season, but rather small proto-figs which drop off, leaving room for the real figs to grow later in the year. But poets leap in where Bible commentators fear to tread.

THE BLASTED FIG

And on the morrow, when they were come from Bethany, he was
hungry: and seeing a fig tree afar off having leaves, he came, if haply
he might find any thing thereon: and when he came to it, he found
nothing but leaves; for the time of figs was not yet. And Jesus
answered and said unto it, No man eat fruit of thee hereafter for
ever. And his disciples heard it . . .

And in the morning, as they passed by, they saw the fig tree
dried up from the roots. And Peter calling to remembrance saith
unto him, Master, behold, the fig tree which thou cursedst is
withered away. And Jesus answering saith unto them, Have faith in
God. For verily I say unto you, That whosoever shall say unto this
mountain, Be thou removed, and be thou cast into the sea; and shall
not doubt in his heart, but shall believe that those things which he
saith shall come to pass; he shall have whatsoever he saith. Therefore
I say unto you, What things soever ye desire, when ye pray, believe
that ye receive them, and ye shall have them.

Mark 11:20–24

THE FIG TREE

Art thou not planted by the water-side?
Know'st not thy Lord by fruit is glorified?
The sentence is, 'Cut down the barren tree!'
Bear fruit, or else thy end will cursèd be!

He, that about thy root takes pains to dig,
Would, if on thee were found but one good fig,
Preserve thee from the axe; but, barren tree,
Bear fruit, or else thy end will cursèd be!

The utmost end of patience is at hand,
'Tis much if thou much longer here doth stand.
O cumber-ground, thou art a barren tree,
Bear fruit, or else thy end will cursèd be!

JOHN BUNYAN (1628–1688)

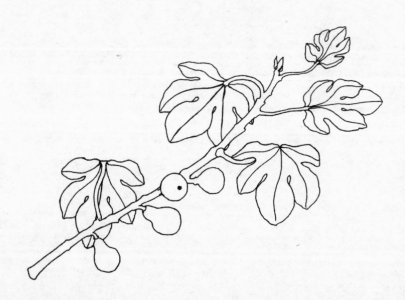

THE PARABLE OF THE FIG TREE

And he spake to them a parable; Behold the fig tree, and all the trees; when they now shoot forth, ye see and know of your own selves that summer is now nigh at hand. So likewise ye, when ye see these things come to pass, know ye that the kingdom of God is nigh at hand.

Luke 21:29–31

130   Beware of false prophets, which come to you in sheep's clothing,
       but inwardly they are ravening wolves. Ye shall know them by their
       fruits. Do men gather grapes of thorns, or figs of thistles? Even so
       every good tree bringeth forth good fruit; but a corrupt tree
       bringeth forth evil fruit. A good tree cannot bring forth evil fruit,
       neither can a corrupt tree bring forth good fruit. Every tree that
       bringeth not forth good fruit is hewn down, and cast into the fire.
       Wherefore by their fruits ye shall know them.

Matthew 7:15-20

An Orange Tree

Oh that I were an orange-tree,
> That busie plant!
Then should I ever laden be,
> And never want
Some fruit for him that dressèd me.

GEORGE HERBERT (1593–1633)
Employment II

ADORATION

For ADORATION seasons change,
And order, truth, and beauty range,
      Adjust, attract, and fill:
The grass the polyanthus cheques;
And polish'd porphyry reflects,
      By the descending rill.

Rich almonds colour to the prime
For ADORATION; tendrils climb,
      And fruit trees pledge their gems;
And Ivis, with her gorgeous vest,
Builds for her eggs her cunning nest,
      And bell-flowers bow their stems.

Now labour his reward receives,
For ADORATION counts his sheaves,
      To peace, her bounteous prince;
The nectarine his strong tint imbibes,
And apples of ten thousand tribes,
      And quick peculiar quince.

CHRISTOPHER SMART (1722–1771)

THE WORLD IS A POMEGRANATE

The World is a pomegranate indeed, which God hath put into man's heart, as Solomon observeth in the Ecclesiastics, because it containeth the seeds of grace and the seeds of glory. All virtues lie in the World, as seeds in a pomegranate: I mean in the fruition of it, out of which when it is sown in man's heart they naturally arise . . .

THOMAS TRAHERNE (1637–1674)

THE ALOE

I

One hundred feet from off the ground
That noble aloe blows;
But mark ye by what skill profound
His charming grandeur rose.

II

One hundred years of patient care
The gardeners did bestow,
Toil and hereditary pray'r
Made all this glorious show.

III

Thus man goes on from year to year,
And bears no fruit at all;
But gracious God, still unsevere,
Bids show'rs of blessings fall.

IV

The beams of mercy, dews of grace,
Our Saviour still supplies –
Ha! ha! the soul regains her place,
And sweetens all the skies.

CHRISTOPHER SMART (1722–1771)
(*Hymn 29 – Long-suffering of God*)

IN THE ORCHARD

THE SPIRITUAL USE OF AN ORCHARD
OR GARDEN OF FRUIT TREES

I shall now consider fruit trees upon another account and endeavour to make some spiritual use and improvement of them. And this should be our care, as to all creatures which we have to do with upon all occasions: according to the example of Our Lord and Saviour whose use it was to spiritualise natural and moral things, when he conversed with us in his bodily presence. And many spiritual things he illustrates by similitudes from natural things . . . from seeds, tares, mustard seeds, leaven, a treasure in the field, a pearl, a draw-net, etc. So should we make a spiritual use of natural things; and so turn earth (as it were) into heaven.

When we have gone through all the works and labours to be performed in the orchard and have received thereby a rich recompence of temporal profits and pleasures in the use of the trees and fruits, we may (besides all that) make a spiritual use of them, and receive more and greater profits and pleasures thereby . . .

. . . The world is a great library, and fruit trees are some of the books wherein we may read and see plainly the attributes of God, his power, wisdom, goodness etc. and be instructed and taught our duty towards him in many things, even from fruit trees: for as trees (in a metaphorical sense) are books, so likewise in the same sense they have a voice, and speak plainly to us, and teach us many good lessons.

As I have planted many thousands of natural fruit trees for the good of the common wealth, so also I have taken some spiritual sciences or profits from them. I mean several propositions drawn from observations in nature, which are somewhat branched forth into boughs and twigs, and sent them abroad for the good of the church of God: and if men will but accept them, and be content to have them engrafted in their own gardens (their hearts and minds) by the Husbandman's watering of them by his Spirit, they will grow and blossom, and bear much good fruit, here and for ever. Fruits of faith, love, joy, peace, and other fruits of the spirit, bunches of grapes for the feeding and refreshing of our souls as we travel through the wilderness, and the increase of our glory hereafter in Canaan to all eternity.

Which improvement the Great Husbandman grant thee, together with

Thy servant in the Lord,

R.A. Austen

RALPH AUSTEN (?c.1600–1676)
From the Preface to *The Spiritual Use of An Orchard or Garden of Fruit Trees*

SOULS ARE LIKE APPLES

. . . My soul was only apt and disposed to great things; but souls to souls are like apples to apples, one being rotten rots another . . .

THOMAS TRAHERNE (1637–1674)

EVE

Eve, with her basket, was
Deep in the bells and grass,
Wading in bells and grass
Up to her knees.
Picking a dish of sweet
Berries and plums to eat,
Down in the bells and grass
Under the trees.

Mute as a mouse in a
Corner the cobra lay,
Curled round a bough of the
Cinnamon tall . . .
Now to get even and
Humble proud heaven and
Now was the moment or
Never at all.

'Eva!' Each syllable
Light as a flower fell,
'Eva!' he whispered the
Wondering maid,
Soft as a bubble sung
Out of a linnet's lung,
Soft and most silverly
'Eva!' he said.

Picture that orchard sprite;
Eve, with her body white,
Supple and smooth to her
Slim finger-tips;
Wondering, listening,
Listening, wondering,
Eve with a berry
Half-way to her lips.

Oh, had our simple Eve
Seen through the make-believe!
Had she but known the
Pretender he was!
Out of the boughs he came,
Whispering still her name,
Tumbling in twenty rings
Into the grass.

Here was the strangest pair
In the world anywhere,
Eve in the bells and grass
Kneeling, and hell
Telling his story low . . .
Singing birds saw them go
Down the dark path to
The Blasphemous Tree.

Oh, what a clatter when
Titmouse and Jenny Wren
Saw him successful and
Taking his leave!
How the birds rated him,
How they all hated him!
How they all pitied
Poor motherless Eve!

Picture her crying
Outside in the lane,
Eve, with no dish of sweet
Berries and plums to eat,
Haunting the gate of the
Orchard in vain . . .
Picture the lewd delight
Under the hill tonight –
'Eva!' the toast goes round,
'Eva!' again.

RALPH HODGSON (1871–1962)

PARADISE

I bless thee, Lord, because I GROW
Among the trees, which in a ROW
To thee both fruit and order OW.

What open force, or hidden CHARM
Can blast my fruit, or bring me HARM,
While the inclosure is thine ARM:

Inclose me still for fear I START;
Be to me rather sharp and TART,
Than let me want thy hand and ART.

When thou dost greater judgments SPARE,
And with thy knife but prune and PARE,
Even fruitful trees more fruitful ARE:

Such sharpness shows the sweetest FREND,
Such cuttings rather heal than REND,
And such beginnings touch their END.

GEORGE HERBERT (1593–1633)

THE PEAR TREE

The weathered pear, four generations old
My window-meditation, lives in peace.
Rough boughs, pale clouds of fragile blossom hold
Where slim bees hover. Tender leaves increase,
Light-fringed, to cup the summer sky and move
In gentle lifting through blue-dappled shade.
So may I ponder on such kindly Love
Which keeps in beauty every shining blade
Destined so soon to drift through Autumn air
Towards Winter dissolution: Glory lost
Reveals new grandeur of trimmed branches, bare
To the gale's strength, crisp outlined in chaste frost.
So wondering, I dream through the tree's year
Learning acceptance of God's Order here.

CLARE GIRLING

Joseph was an old man,
    And an old man was he,
When he wedded Mary
    In the land of Galilee.

Joseph and Mary walked
    Through an orchard good,
Where was cherries and berries
    So red as any blood.

Joseph and Mary walked
    Through an orchard green,
Where was berries and cherries
    As thick as might be seen.

O then bespoke Mary,
    With words so meek and mild,
'Pluck me one cherry, Joseph,
    For I am now with child.'

O then bespoke Joseph,
    With answer most unkind,
'Let him pluck thee a cherry
    That brought thee now with child.'

O then bespoke the baby
    Within his mother's womb –
'Bow down then the tallest tree
    For my mother to have some.'

Then bowed down the highest tree,
    Unto his mother's hand.
Then she cried, 'See, Joseph,
    I have cherries at command.'

O then bespake Joseph –
    'I have done Mary wrong;
But now cheer up, my dearest,
    And do not be cast down.

'O eat your cherries, Mary,
    O eat your cherries now,
O eat your cherries, Mary,
    That grow upon the bough.'

Then Mary plucked a cherry,
    As red as any blood;
Then Mary she went homewards
    All with her heavy load.

TRADITIONAL

THE EXPECTATION

Over the apple-trees with their red load
In world's-end orchards, over dark yew woods,
O'er fires of sunset glassed in wizard streams,
O'er mill and meadow of those farthest lands,
Over the reapers, over the sere sails
Of homing ships and every breaking wave,
Over the haven and the entrancèd town,
O'er hearths aflame with fire-trunks and fir-cones,
Over the children playing in the streets,
Over the harpers harping on the bridge,
O'er lovers in their dream and their desire,
There falls from the high heaven a subtle sense
Of presage and a deep, expectant hush,
And the wise watchers know the time draws on
And that amid the snows of that same year
The earth will bear her longed-for perfect Fruit.

RICHARD LAWSON GALES

THE CROSS OF CHRIST

' . . . Who by the tree of the Cross didst give salvation unto
mankind: that whence death arose, thence life might rise again:
and that He, Who by a tree overcame, might also by a tree be
overcome . . . ' *Preface of the Holy Cross*

God in pity saw man fallen,
    Shamed and sunk in misery,
When he fell on death by tasting
    Fruit of the forbidden tree;
Then another tree was chosen
    Which the world from death should free.

BISHOP FORTUNATUS (1st century)

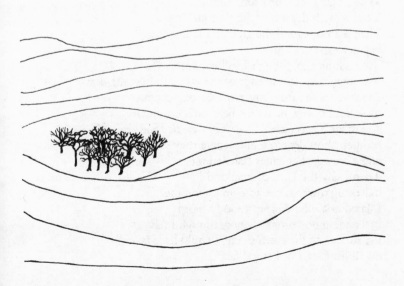

THE DREAM OF THE ROOD

Listen! I will tell of a marvellous dream
which came to me in the middle of the night,
while the rest of the world was asleep in bed.
It was as if I saw a wondrous tree,
high in the sky, surrounded with light –
the brightest of beams. Like a beacon, it was all
covered with gold; beautiful gems gleamed
at the corner of the earth, as well as the five
upon the cross-beam. Hosts of angels,
fair for all time, looked on. It was by no means a thieves' gallows,
for holy spirits, and mankind, and all creation
gazed on the glorious tree,
I, though, was stained with my sins,
pierced with guilt. But I saw the glorious tree
shining brilliantly in rich attire, decked with gold.
The Creator's tree was magnificently adorned with gems.
But through that gold, I could see
the wretched agony once suffered there,
as blood began to seep on its right side.
I was filled with sorrow and fear,
even at so fair a sight. I saw the shining beacon
changing its adornment and colour: sometimes
it was covered with blood and dripping with gore;
sometimes decked with treasure.
While I lay there for a long time,
looking with distress at the Saviour's tree,
I heard a noise, and the greatest of all woods
began to speak to me:
'It was long ago, though I still remember,
that men came to the edge of the wood to hew me down
and remove me from my roots. Strong enemies
took hold of me, made me bear their criminals
and made a spectacle of me. They carried me
on their shoulders to a hill, where they set me,
and a crowd of enemies fastened me.
Then I saw the Lord of mankind
hastening towards me, to climb upon me.
I dared not offend against God's word
by bending down or breaking, though I felt
the surface of the earth shake. I could have fallen
on all his foes, but I stood fast.

Then that young hero (who was God Almighty)
prepared himself, strong and resolute.
He climbed up into the gallows-tree,
bold before such a crowd, for he wished to save mankind.
I shook as the warrior embraced me,
but again, I dared not bend to the ground
or fall to the earth. I had to stand firm.
A rood, I was raised up, and I raised up the noble King,
the Lord of Heaven, and could not bow down.
They drove dark nails through me,
and the wounds can still be seen, deep marks of hatred.
Yet I dared not hurt any of them.
They mocked both of us together.
I was all drenched with blood, which poured from the man's side.
Then He set his Spirit free.
Afterwards, I had to endure many cruel things on that hill-top.
I saw the God of hosts stretched out brutally.
Darkness came, and clouds shrouded the Lord's body;
as shadows gathered, the black clouds
obscured his shining radiance. All creation wept,
lamenting the King's fall. Christ was on the cross.
Then I saw people running from afar
to their Lord. I watched it all.
I was weak with so much sorrow, yet eagerly and humbly
I let him down into their hands. They picked up Almighty God,
lifting him from his heavy torment.
The soldiers left me standing there, soaked
and wounded all over with sharp metal.
They laid the body down, heavy limbed,
And then stood by his head, looking down on the King of heaven.
And he rested there a while, tired after so long a struggle.
Then they began to make a tomb for him in sight of me,
carving it from bright stone.
They placed the king of victory inside.
Then they began to sing a dirge, sorrowful in the evening.
And, weary, they turned away, leaving their noble Lord all alone.
But we remained there, weeping in that place
for a long while after the soldiers' voices had faded.
The fair body grew cold. Then we were cut down,
a fearful fate. We were buried in a deep pit.
But the Lord's friends and servants discovered where I was,

148   And adorned me with gold and silver.
       Now you can understand, dear warrior,
       what deeds, what deep sorrows, I have suffered
       at the hands of wicked men. Now, though,
       the time has come for men from far and wide to honour me;
       and for the whole of this marvellous creation
       to offer praise to this beacon. On me
       the Son of God once suffered; therefore I stretch gloriously
       across the heavens. And I have power to heal
       all those who live in awe of me.
       Once, I was the cruellest of all punishments,
       most hated by men. That was before I became the gate
       to the way of life for everyone.
       Then the Prince of glory raised me up,
       and the King of heaven placed me above all other trees,
       just as almighty God exalted his mother, Mary,
       above all other women, for everyone to worship.
       Now I command you, dear warrior,
       to pass on this vision to all people.
       Pronounce the words, that this is the tree of glory . . .

                                    ANONYMOUS (c. 8th century)
                                    Translated by Paul Handley

BLAME

. . . There grew a goodly tree him faire beside,
    Loaden with fruit and apples rosie red,
    As they in pure vermilion had beene dide,
    Whereof great vertues over all were red:
    For happie life to all, which thereon fed,
    And life eke everlasting did befall:
    Great God it planted in that blessed sted
    With his almightie hand, and did it call
The tree of life, the crime of our first father's fall.

In all the world like was not to be found,
    Save in that soile, where all good things did grow,
    And freely sprong out of the fruitfull ground,
    As incorrupted Nature did them sow,
    Till that dread Dragon all did overthrow.
    Another like faire tree eke grew thereby,
    Whereof who so did eat, eftsoones did know
    Both good and ill: O mornefull memory:
That tree through one man's fault hath doen us all to dy.

From that first tree forth flowd, as from a well,
    A trickling streame of Balme, most soveraine
    And daintie deare, which on the ground still fell,
    And overflowèd all the fertill plaine,
    And it had deawèd bene with timely raine:
    Life and long health that gratious ointment gave,
    And deadly woundes could heale, and reare againe
    The senselesse corse appointed for the grave.
Into that same he fell: which did from death him save . . .

EDMUND SPENSER (1552–1599)

Some folk as can afford,
So I've heard say,
Set up a sort of cross
Right in the garden way
To mind 'em of the Lord.

But I, when I do see
Thik apple tree
An' stoopin' limb
All spread wi' moss,
I think of Him
And how He talks wi' me.

I think of God
And how He trod
That garden long ago;
He walked, I reckon, to and fro
And then sat down
Upon the groun'
Or some low limb
What suited Him
Such as you see
On many a tree,
And on thik very one
Where I at set o' sun
Do sit and talk wi' He.

And, mornings too, I rise and come
An' sit down where the branch be low;
And birds do sing, a bee do hum,
The flowers in the border blow,
And all my heart's so glad and clear
As pools when mists do disappear:
As pools a-laughing in the light
When mornin' air is swep' an' bright,
As pools what got all Heaven in sight
So's my heart's cheer
When He be near.

He never pushed the garden door,
He left no footmark on the floor;
I never heard 'Un stir nor tread
And yet His Hand do bless my head,
And when 'tis time for work to start
I takes Him with me in my heart.

And when I die, pray God I see
At very last thik apple tree
An' stoopin' limb,
And think of Him
And all He been to me.

ANNA BUNSTON

152

The tree of life my soul hath seen,
Laden with fruit, and always green:
The trees of nature fruitless be
Compared with Christ the apple tree.

His beauty doth all things excell:
By faith I know, but ne'er can tell
The glory which I now can see
In Jesus Christ the apple tree.

For happiness I long have sought,
And pleasure dearly I have bought:
I missed of all; but now I see
'Tis found in Christ the apple tree.

I'm weary with my former toil,
Here I will sit and rest awhile:
Under the shadow I will be,
Of Jesus Christ the apple tree.

This fruit doth make my soul to thrive,
It keeps my dying faith alive;
Which makes my soul in haste to be
With Jesus Christ the apple tree.

Divine Hymns or Spiritual Songs,
compiled by Joshua Smith, New Hampshire, 1784

A CIDER SONG

*Extract from a Romance which is not yet
written and probably never will be.*

The wine they drink in Paradise
They make in Haute Lorraine;
God brought it burning from the sod
To be a sign and signal rod
That they that drink the blood of God
Shall never thirst again.

The wine they praise in Paradise
They make in Ponterey,
The purple wine of Paradise,
But we have better at the price;
It's wine they praise in Paradise,
It's cider that they pray.

The wine they want in Paradise
They find in Plodder's End,
The apple wine of Hereford,
Of Hafod Hill and Hereford,
Where woods went down to Hereford,
And there I had a friend.

The soft feet of the blessed go
In the soft western vales,
The road the silent saints accord,
The road from Heaven to Hereford,
Where the apple wood of Hereford
Goes all the way to Wales.

G.K. CHESTERTON (1874–1936)

154

On eating Fruit which grows on Trees:

Blessed art thou, O Lord our God, King of the universe, who createst the fruit of the tree.

On eating Fruit which grows on the Ground:

Blessed art thou, O Lord our God, King of the universe, who createst the fruit of the earth.

On smelling Fragrant Woods or Barks:

Blessed art thou, O Lord our God, King of the universe, who createst fragrant woods.

On smelling Odorous Plants:

Blessed art thou, O Lord our God, King of the universe, who createst odorous plants.

On smelling Odorous Fruits:

Blessed art thou, O Lord our God, King of the universe, who givest a goodly scent to fruits.

On smelling Fragrant Spices:

Blessed art thou, O Lord our God, King of the universe, who createst divers kinds of spices.

On smelling Fragrant Oils:

Blessed art thou, O Lord our God, King of the universe, who createst fragrant oil.

On seeing Beautiful Trees or Animals:

Blessed art thou, O Lord our God, King of the universe, who hast such as these in thy world.

On seeing Trees blossoming the first time in the Year:

Blessed art thou, O Lord our God, King of the universe, who hast made thy world lacking in nought, but hast produced therein goodly creatures and goodly trees wherewith to give delight unto the children of men.

THE SCARECROW

In the abandoned orchard – on a pole,
The rain-soaked trappings of that scarecrow have
Usurped the semblance of a man – poor soul –
    Haled from a restless grave.

Geese for his company this fog-bound noon,
He eyeless stares. And I with eyes reply.
Lifting a snakelike head, the gander yelps
    'Ware!' at the passer-by.

It is as though a few bedraggled rags
Poised in this wintry waste were lure enough
To entice some aimless phantom here to mime
    All it is image of . . .

Once Man in grace divine all beauty was;
And of his bone God made a lovelier Eve;
Now even the seraphs sleep at sentry-go;
    The swine break in to thieve

Wind-fallen apples from the two old Trees.
Oh see, Old Adam, once of Eden! Alas!
How is thy beauty fallen: fallen thine Eve,
    Who did all life surpass!

Should in the coming nightfall the Lord God,
Goose-challenged, call, 'My Creature, where art *thou*?'
Scarecrow of hate and vengeance, wrath and blood,
    What would'st thou answer now?

WALTER DE LA MARE (1873–1956)

156

God, in the whizzing of a pleasant wind,
Shall march upon the tops of mulberry trees.

GEORGE PEELE (?1558–?1597)

TO THE FIELDS

THE PATH

See'st thou that path, which ever since
    With lilies and with violets hath smiled,
Sweetly acknowledging the influence
Both of the passing mother and the child?
    The country wondered at the beauteous list,
    But from whose feet it sprung, they little wist.

As to the sea the silver river through
A thousand by-paths steals its secret way,
So doth this flowery track to Egypt flow,
Declining all things that its course might stay.
    Doubt not the windings, but securely ride,
    For now the way itself's thy fragrant guide.

JOSEPH BEAUMONT

THE LILIES OF THE FIELD

Consider the lilies of the field, how they grow; they toil not, neither do they spin: and yet I say unto you, That even Solomon in all his glory was not arrayed like one of these. Wherefore, if God so clothe the grass of the field, which today is, and tomorrow is cast into the oven, shall he not much more clothe you, O ye of little faith?

Matthew 6:28–30

GOD PROVIDETH FOR THE MORROW

Lo, the lilies of the field,
How their leaves instruction yield!
Hark to nature's lesson given
By the blessed birds of heaven!
Every bush and tufted tree
Warbles sweet philosophy: –
Mortal, flee from doubt and sorrow:
GOD provideth for the morrow!

Say, with richer crimson glows
The kingly mantle than the rose?
Say, have kings more wholesome fare
Than we poor citizens of air?
Barns nor hoarded grain have we,
Yet we carol merrily; –
Mortal, flee from doubt and sorrow;
GOD provideth for the morrow!

One there lives whose guardian eye
Guides our humble destiny:
ONE there lives, who, Lord of all,
Keeps our feathers lest they fall:
Pass we blithely, then, the time,
Fearless of the snare and lime,
Free from doubt and faithless sorrow;
GOD provideth for the morrow!

REGINALD HEBER (1783–1826)

CONSIDER THE LILIES

Behold, O man, that toilsome pains dost take,
The flowers, the fields, and all that pleasant grows,
How they themselves do thine ensample make,
Whiles nothing-envious nature them forth throws
Out of her fruitful lap; how, no man knows,
They spring, they bud, they blossom fresh and fair,
And deck the world with their rich pompous shows;
Yet no man for them taketh pains or care,
Yet no man to them can his careful pains compare.

The lily, lady of the flowering field,
The flower-de-luce, her lovely paramour,
Bid thee to them thy fruitless labours yield,
And soon leave off this toilsome weary stour:
Lo! lo, how brave she decks her bounteous bower,
With silken curtains and gold coverlets,
Therein to shroud her sumptuous belamour,
Yet neither spins nor cards, nor cares nor frets,
But to her mother nature all her care she lets.

EDMUND SPENSER (1552–1599)

VEGETATION

O never harm the dreaming world,
the world of green, the world of leaves,
but let its million palms unfold
the adoration of the trees.

It is a love in darkness wrought
obedient to the unseen sun,
longer than memory, a thought
deeper than the graves of time.

The turning spindles of the cells
weave a slow forest over space,
the dance of love, creation,
out of time moves not a leaf,
and out of summer, not a shade.

KATHLEEN RAINE (b. 1908)

THE VOICE OF GOD

I bent again unto the ground,
And I heard the quiet sound
Which the grasses make when they
Come up laughing from the clay.

We are the voice of God! they said:
Thereupon I bent my head
Down again that I might see
If they truly spoke to me.

But, around me, everywhere
Grass and tree and mountain were
Thundering in mighty glee,
We are the voice of Deity!

And I leapt from where I lay:
I danced upon the laughing clay:
And, to the rock that sang beside,
We are the voice of God! I cried.

JAMES STEPHENS (1882–1950)

164 A child said, What is the grass? fetching it to me with full hands;
How could I answer the child? I do not know what it is any more
than he.

I guess it must be the flag of my disposition, out of hopeful green
stuff woven.

Or I guess it is the handkerchief of the Lord,
A scented gift and remembrancer designedly dropt,
Bearing the owner's name someway in the corners, that we may see
and remark, and *Whose?*

Or I guess the grass is itself a child, the produced babe of the
vegetation.

Or I guess it is a uniform hieroglyphic,
And it means, Sprouting alike in broad zones and narrow zones.

Growing among black folks as among white,
Kanuck, Tuckahoe, Congressman, Cuff, I give them the same, I
receive them the same.

And now it seems to me the beautiful uncut hair of graves.

Tenderly will I use you curling grass.
It may be you transpire from the breasts of young men,
It may be if I had known them I would have loved them,
It may be you are from old people, or from offspring taken soon out
of their mothers' laps,

And here you are the mothers' laps.
This grass is very dark to be from the white heads of old mothers,
Darker than the colourless beards of old men,
Dark to come from under the faint red roofs of mouths.
O I perceive after all so many uttering tongues,
And I perceive they do not come from the roofs of mouths for
nothing.

I wish I could translate the hints about the dead young men and
women,
And the hints about old men and mothers, and the offspring taken
soon out of their laps.

What do you think has become of the young and old men?
And what do you think has become of the women and children?

They are alive and well somewhere,
The smallest sprout shows there is really no death,
And if ever there was it led forward life, and does not wait at the
    end to arrest it,
And ceased the moment life appeared.

All goes onward and outward, nothing collapses,
And to die is different from what any one supposed, and luckier.

WALT WHITMAN (1819–1892)
Song of Myself

HOW MANY HEAVENS

The emeralds are singing on the grasses
And in the trees the bells of the long cold are ringing, –
My blood seems changed to emeralds like the spears
Of grass beneath the earth piercing and singing.

The flame of the first blade
Is an angel piercing through the earth to sing
'God is everything!'

'The grass within the grass, the angel in the angel, flame
Within the flame, and He is the green shade that came
To be the heart of shade.'

The grey-beard angel of the stone,
Who has grown wise with age, cried 'Not alone
Am I within my silence, – God is the stone in the still stone,
    the silence laid
In the heart of silence' . . . then, above the glade

The yellow straws of light
Whereof the sun has built his nest, cry 'Bright
Is the world, the yellow straw
My brother, – God is the straw within the straw: –
        All things are Light.'

He is the sea of ripeness and the sweet apple's emerald lore.
So you, my flame of grass, my root of the world from which
    all Spring shall grow,
O you, my hawthorn bough of the stars, now leaning low
Through the day, for your flowers to kiss my lips, shall know
He is the core of the heart of love, and He, beyond
    labouring seas, our ultimate shore.

EDITH SITWELL (1887–1964)

THE CHILD'S VISION

The corn was orient and immortal wheat, which never should be reaped, nor was ever sown. I thought it had stood from everlasting to everlasting. The dust and stones of the street were as precious as gold: the gates were at first the end of the world. The green trees when I saw them first through one of the gates transported and ravished me, their sweetness and unusual beauty made my heart to leap, and almost mad with ecstasy, they were such strange and wonderful things.

THOMAS TRAHERNE (1637–1674)
Centuries of Meditations

Now, before the wheat
Standing so nobly, falls:
Ere yet the first owl calls,
Or that thin sickle and fleet
Of harvest moon her earliest quarter passes,
Or the ground-frost may crisp the twice-mown grasses:
Now let me sing
My quiet stave, when redbreast too
Sings in, as I beneath, the yew:
Before they bring
The apples home, and once again
The equinox beats down the leaves in rain.

We had thought summer dead:
Year upon year
Prone in the furrow lay the smutted ear;
More wan than red
Hung tasteless fruit; flowers made earth their bier:
Kine to the lowering sky
Frowned in mute patience, and the hooded hind
Driving them home, in the soft ruts plodded by
With streaming shoulders and a heart unkind,
Sullen and bowed
Against a swagging heap of swollen cloud.

But now hot camomile in headlands grows,
Coarse-smelling as from toil of reaping; bees
Their delicate harvest in the rusty rows
Of scarlet bean, and woodbine that still blows,
Though flower with berry, gather and do not cease:
No mushroom yet, for dryness of the leas:
No leaf too early sere, for droughty root,
Drops from the trees,
But grave broad green guards the thick purple fruit.

Not only thanks for ample grain,
And apple that shall give her wine
As in old seasons, strong again;
Nor for low streams where lilies shine
In many a pool unvexed by flood,
Unvexed by aught but boys at play:
Not only for the sun in the blood
And the long, blest, eventless day;

But chiefly for the sign,
For the fair time was token of grace
That life is yet benign,
That this our race
Still doth possess a pleasant place:
For many a doubt
Assails us, and might overthrow,
Were not the bow
Of blessing high in heaven hung out;
Our time is dark,
And save such miracle as this
Where is the mark
To steer by, in our bitter mysteries?

RUTH PITTER (b. 1897)

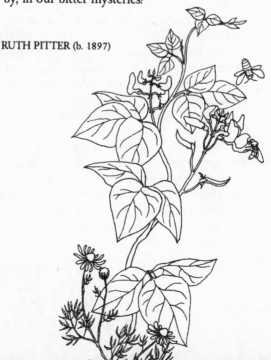

170   Except a corn of wheat fall into the ground and die, it abideth alone:
       but if it die, it bringeth forth much fruit. He that loveth his life shall
       lose it; and he that hateth his life in this world shall keep it unto life
       eternal.

John 12:24–25

WHEAT

If you will look at a grain of wheat you will see that it seems folded
up: it has crossed its arms and rolled itself up in a cloak, a fold of
which forms a groove, and so gone to sleep. If you look at it some
time, as people in the old enchanted days used to look into a mirror,
or the magic ink, until they saw living figures therein, you can
almost trace a miniature human being in the oval of the grain. It is
narrow at the top, where the head would be, and broad across the
shoulders, and narrow again down towards the feet; a tiny man or
woman has wrapped itself round about with a garment and settled
down to slumber. Up in the far north, where the dead ice reigns,
our arctic explorers used to roll themselves in a sleeping-bag like this,
to keep the warmth in their bodies against the chilliness of the night.
Down in the south, where the heated sands of Egypt never cool,
there in the rock-hewn tombs lie the mummies wrapped and lapped
and wound about with a hundred yards of linen, in the hope, it may
be, that spices and balm might retain within the sarcophagus some
small fragment of human organism through endless ages, till at last
the gift of life revisited it. Like a grain of wheat the mummy is
folded in its cloth. And I do not know really whether I might not
say that these little grains of English corn do not hold within them
the actual flesh and blood of man. Transubstantiation is a fact there.

RICHARD JEFFERIES (1848–1887)
Field and Hedgerow

THE FIELD OF THE SLOTHFUL

I went by the field of the slothful,
And by the vineyard of the man void of understanding;
And, lo, it was all grown over with thorns,
And nettles had covered the face thereof,
And the stone wall thereof was broken down.
Then I saw, and considered it well:
I looked upon it, and received instruction.

Proverbs 24:30–32

'. . . Along the road Christ led me forth.'

So up the road I wander slow
Past where the snowdrops used to grow
With celandines in early springs,
When rainbows were triumphant things
And dew so bright and flowers so glad,
Eternal joy to lass and lad.
And past the lovely brook I paced,
The brook whose source I never traced,
The brook, the one of two which rise
In my green dream in Paradise,
In wells where heavenly buckets clink
To give God's wandering thirsty drink
By those clean cots of carven stone
Where the clear water sings alone.
Then down, past that white-blossomed pond,
And past the chestnut trees beyond,
And past the bridge the fishers knew,
Where yellow flag flowers once grew,
Where we'd go gathering cops of clover,
In sunny June times long since over.
O clover-cops half white, half red,
O beauty from beyond the dead.
O blossom, key to earth and heaven,
O souls that Christ has new forgiven . . .

. . . Slow up the hill the plough team plod,
Old Callow at the task of God,
Helped by man's wit, helped by the brute
Turning a stubborn clay to fruit,
His eyes for ever on some sign
To help him plough a perfect line.
At top of rise the plough team stopped,
The fore-horse bent his head and cropped.
Then the chains chack, the brasses jingle,
The lean reins gather through the cringle,
The figures move against the sky,
The clay wave breaks as they go by.
I kneeled there in the muddy fallow,

I knew that Christ was there with Callow,
That Christ was standing there with me,
That Christ had taught me what to be,
That I should plough, and as I ploughed
My Saviour Christ would sing aloud,
And as I drove the clods apart
Christ would be ploughing in my heart,
Through rest-harrow and bitter roots,
Through all my bad life's rotten fruits.

O Christ who holds the open gate,
O Christ who drives the furrow straight,
O Christ, the plough, O Christ, the laughter
Of holy white birds flying after,
Lo, all my heart's field red and torn,
And Thou wilt bring the young green corn
The young green corn divinely springing,
The young green corn for ever singing;
And when the field is fresh and fair
Thy blessed feet shall glitter there.
And we will walk the weeded field,
And tell the golden harvest's yield,
The corn that makes the holy bread
By which the soul of man is fed,
The holy bread, the food unpriced,
The everlasting mercy, Christ.

JOHN MASEFIELD (1878–1967)

174

He rode at furious speed to Broken Edge,
And he was very angry, very small;
But God was kind, knowing he needed not
A scolding, nor a swift unpleasant fall,
Nor any high reproach of soul at all.
'It matters not,' said Reason and Good Sense;
'Absurd to let a trifle grow immense.'
'It matters very much,' said Busy Brain;
'You cannot be content and calm again,
For you are angry in a righteous cause.'
'Poor, queer old Waxy!' laughed the hips and haws.
'God has a sense of humour,' said a ball
Of orange-gold inside a spindle-berry –
'And "Christ our Lorde is full exceeding merrie".'

He lingered in the lane at Broken Edge,
Bryony berries burned from every hedge;
Snails in the deep wet grass of fairy rings
Told him of unimaginable things.
Love was in all the colours of the sky,
Love in the folded shadows of the high
Blue hills, as quiet as any Easter Eve.
(O fool, O blind and earthbound thus to grieve!)

He turned his horse. Through level sunset-gleams
He saw a sudden little road that curled
And climbed elusive to a sky of dreams.
His anger over Broken Edge was hurled
To scatter into nothing on a gust
Of wind which brought the twilight to the trees.
The drifted leaves, the white October dust
Hiding the beechnuts for the squirrels' store,
Heard the low whisper spoken on his knees: –
'God, You have made a very perfect world,
Don't let me spoil it ever any more.'

V.L. EDMINSON

PARABLES IN THE FIELDS

Behold, a sower went forth to sow; and when he sowed, some seeds fell by the way side, and the fowls came and devoured them up: some fell upon stony places, where they had not much earth: and forthwith they sprung up, because they had no deepness of earth: and when the sun was up, they were scorched; and because they had no root, they withered away. And some fell among thorns; and the thorns sprung up, and choked them: but others fell into good ground, and brought forth fruit, some an hundredfold, some sixtyfold, some thirtyfold. Who hath ears to hear, let him hear . . .

Hear ye therefore the parable of the sower. When any one heareth the word of the kingdom, and understandeth it not, then cometh the wicked one, and catcheth away that which was sown in his heart. This is he which received seed by the way side. But he that received the seed into stony places, the same is he that heareth the word, and anon with joy receiveth it; yet hath he not root in himself, but dureth for a while: for when tribulation or persecution ariseth because of the word, by and by he is offended. He also that receiveth seed among the thorns is he that heareth the word; and the care of this world, and the deceitfulness of riches, choke the word, and he becometh unfruitful. But he that receiveth seed into the good ground is he that heareth the word, and understandeth it; which also beareth fruit, and bringeth forth, some an hundredfold, some sixty, some thirty.

Another parable put he forth unto them, saying, The kingdom of heaven is likened unto a man which sowed good seed in his field: but while men slept, his enemy came and sowed tares among the wheat, and went his way. But when the blade was sprung up, and brought forth fruit, then appeared the tares also. So the servants of the householder came and said unto him, Sir, didst not thou sow good seed in thy field? from whence then hath it tares? He said unto them, An enemy hath done this. The servants said unto him, Wilt thou then that we go and gather them up? But he said, Nay; lest while ye gather up the tares, ye root up also the wheat with them. Let both grow together until the harvest: and in the time of harvest I will say to the reapers, Gather ye together first the tares, and bind them in bundles to burn them: but gather the wheat into my barn.

Another parable put he forth unto them, saying, The kingdom of heaven is like to a grain of mustard seed, which a man took, and sowed in his field: which indeed is the least of all seeds: but when it is grown, it is the greatest among herbs, and becometh a tree, so that the birds of the air come and lodge in the branches thereof.

Matthew 13:3–9, 18–32

176   It is not causeless, Christ did use compare
          Man's mind unto the soil that tillèd is;
          They both full well indeed agree in this,
          Untillèd, they unfruitful are and bare.
Such seed as is bestowed, they do receive,
          And both yield fruit as God doth give increase;
          Some seed is spilt, some Satan doth bereave,
          Some prosper and produce a plenteous peace;
And as devouring fowls do never cease,
          Nor worms, nor swine, to seek do never miss
          Each one to spoil a part, whilst ploughman his
          Due recompense of pains cannot possess;
             So doth the soul, though tilled with studious care,
             Great store of weeds bring forth, good fruits full rare.

HENRY LOK

PRAYER

God stir the soil,
Run the ploughshare deep,
Cut the furrows round and round,
Overturn the hard, dry ground,
Spare no strength nor toil,
Even though I weep.
In the loose, fresh mangled earth
Sow new seed.
Free of withered vine and weed
Bring fair flowers to birth.

ANONYMOUS

178

Christ's church is likened by him to a field
Which tares and wheat confusedly doth yield;
And he commandeth us to let both grow
Together till the harvest, lest that now
By hasty separation, e'er the day,
We, not good husbands, but the wild boars play,
Rooting up both, whereas they both should stand,
And wait the weeding of the angels' hand.

THOMAS WASHBOURNE (1606–1687)

SEED

From star to star, from sun and spring and leaf,
and almost audible flowers whose sound is silence,
and in the common meadows, springs the seed of life.

Now the lilies open, and the rose
released by summer from the harmless graves
that, centuries deep, are in the air we breathe,
and in our earth, and in our daily bread.

External and innate dimensions hold
the living forms, but not the force of life;
for that interior and holy tree
that in the heart of hearts outlives the world
spreads earthly shade into eternity.

KATHLEEN RAINE (b. 1908)

LOVE IS COME AGAIN

Now the green blade riseth from the buried grain,
Wheat that in dark earth many days has lain;
Love lives again, that with the dead has been:

Love is come again,
Like wheat that springeth green.

In the grave they laid him, Love whom men had slain,
Thinking that never he would wake again,
Laid in the earth like grain that sleeps unseen:

Forth he came at Easter, like the risen grain,
He that for three days in the grave had lain,
Quick from the dead my risen Lord is seen:

When our hearts are wintry, grieving, or in pain,
Thy touch can call us back to life again,
Fields of our hearts that dead and bare have been:

J.M.C. CRUM

SPRING

Nothing is so beautiful as spring –
    When weeds, in wheels, shoot long and lovely and lush;
    Thrush's eggs look little low heavens, and thrush
Through the echoing timber does so rinse and wring
The ear, it strikes like lightnings to hear him sing;
    The glassy pear-tree leaves and blooms, they brush
    The descending blue; that blue is all in a rush
With richness; the racing lambs too have fair their fling.

What is all this juice and all this joy?
    A strain of the earth's sweet being in the beginning
In Eden garden. – Have, get, before it cloy,
    Before it cloud, Christ, lord, and sour with sinning,
Innocent mind and Mayday in girl and boy,
    Most, O Maid's child, thy choice and worthy the winning.

GERARD MANLEY HOPKINS (1844–1889)

Say, earth, why hast thou got thee new attire,
And stick'st thy habit full of daisies red?
Seems that thou dost to some high thought aspire,
And some new-found-out bridegroom means't to wed:
Tell me, ye trees, so fresh apparellèd, –
  So never let the spiteful canker waste you,
  So never let the heavens with lightening blast you, –
Why go you now so trimly dressed, or whither haste you?

Answer me, Jordan, why thy crooked tide
So often wanders from his nearest way,
As though some other way thy stream would slide,
And fain salute the place where something lay.
And you, sweet birds that, shaded from the ray,
  Sit carolling and piping grief away,
  The while the lambs to hear you, dance and play,
Tell me, sweet birds, what is it you so fain would say?

And thou, fair spouse of earth, that every year
Gett'st such a numerous issue of thy bride,
How chance thou hotter shin'st, and draw'st more near?
Sure thou somewhere some worthy sight hast spied,
That in one place for joy thou canst not bide:
  And you, dead swallows, that so lively now
  Through the flit air your wingèd passage row,
How could new life into your frozen ashes flow?

Ye primroses and purple violets,
Tell me, why blaze ye from your leavy bed,
And woo men's hands to rent you from your sets,
As though you would somewhere be carrièd,
With fresh perfumes, and velvets garnishèd?
  But ah! I need not ask, 'tis surely so,
  You all would to your Saviour's triumphs go,
There would ye all await, and humble homage do.

GILES FLETCHER (?1588–1623)

SONG OF THE MAYERS

Remember us poor Mayers all,
    And thus we do begin,
To lead our lives in righteousness,
    Or else we die in sin.

We have been rambling all the night,
    And almost all the day,
And now returning back again,
    We have brought you a bunch of May.

A bunch of May we have brought you,
    And at your door it stands,
It is but a sprout, but it's well budded out
    By the work of our Lord's hands.

The hedges and trees they are so green,
    As green as any leek,
Our Heavenly Father, He watered them
    With his heavenly dew so sweet.

The heavenly gates are open wide,
    Our paths are beaten plain,
And if a man be not too far gone,
    He may return again.

The life of man is but a span,
    It flourishes like a flower;
We are here to-day, and gone to-morrow,
    And are dead in an hour.

The moon shines bright, and the stars give a light,
    A little before it is day,
God bless you all, both great and small,
    And send you a joyful May.

TRADITIONAL

184

By the breath of the blue that shines in silence o'er me,
By the length of the mountain lines that stretch before me,
By the height of the cloud that sails, with rest in motion,
Over the plains and the vales to the measureless ocean,
(O, how the sight of the things that are great enlarges the eyes!)
Draw me away from myself to the peace of the hills and the skies.

While the tremulous leafy haze on the woodland is spreading,
And the bloom on the meadow betrays where May has been
    treading;
While the birds on the branches above, and the brooks flowing
    under,
Are singing together of love in a world full of wonder,
(Lo, in the marvel of spring-time, dreams are changed into truth!)
Quicken my heart, and restore the beautiful hopes of youth.

By the faith that the flow'rs show when they bloom unbidden,
By the calm of the river's flow to a goal that is hidden,
By the trust of the tree that clings to its deep foundation,
By the courage of wild birds' wings on the long migration,
(Wonderful secret of peace that abideth in Nature's breast!)
Teach me how to confide, and live my life, and rest.

For the comforting warmth of the sun that my body embraces,
For the cool of the waters that run thro' the shadowy places,
For the balm of the breezes that brush my face with their fingers,
For the vesper hymn of the thrush when the twilight lingers,
Now with a breath that is deep-drawn, breath of a heart without
    care,
I will give thanks and adore thee, God of the open air!

HENRY VAN DYKE (1852–1933)

In Woods

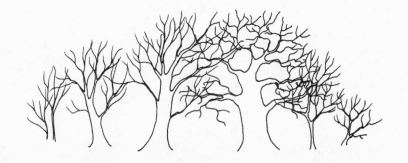

186   Almighty One, in the woods I am blessed. Happy everyone in the
        woods. Every tree speaks through Thee. O God! What glory in the
        woodland! On the heights is peace – peace to serve Him.

                    LUDWIG VAN BEETHOVEN (1770–1827)

MAY IN THE GREEN-WOOD

In somer when the shawes by sheyne,
    And leves be large and long,
Hit is full merry in feyre foreste
    To here the foulys song.

To se the dere draw to the dale
    And leve the lilles hee,
And shadow him in the leves grene
    Under the green-wode tree.

Hit befell on Whitsontide
    Early in a May mornyng,
The Sonne up faire can shyne,
    And the briddis mery can syng.

'This is a mery mornyng,' said Litulle Johne,
    'Be Hym that dyed on tre;
A more mery man than I am one
    Lyves ont in Christiantè.

'Pluk up thi hert, my dere mayster,'
    Litulle Johne can say,
'And thynk hit is a fulle fayre tyme
    In a mornynge of May.'

ANONYMOUS (15th century)

188

Not of áll my eyes see, wandering on the world,
Is anything a milk to the mind so, so sighs deep
Poetry tó it, as a tree whose boughs break in the sky.
Say it is ásh-boughs: whether on a December day and furled
Fast ór they in clammyish lashtender combs creep
Apart wide and new-nestle at heaven most high.
They touch heaven, tabour on it; how their talons sweep
The smouldering enormous winter welkin! May
Mells blue and snow white through them, a fringe and fray
Of greenery: it is old earth's groping towards the steep
         Heaven whom she childs us by.

GERARD MANLEY HOPKINS (1844–1889)

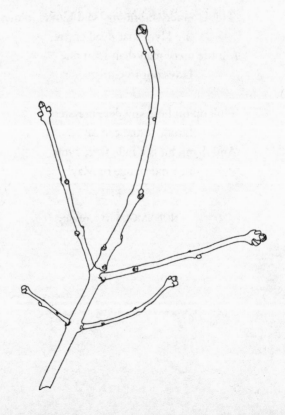

BINSLEY POPLARS

My aspens dear, whose airy cages quelled,
Quelled or quenched in leaves the leaping sun,
All felled, felled, are all felled;
    Of a fresh and following folded rank
        Not spared, not one
        That dandled a sandalled
    Shadow that swam or sank
On meadow and river and wind-wandering weed-winding bank.

O if we but knew what we do
      When we delve or hew –
    Hack and rack the growing green!
      Since country is so tender
    To touch, her being só slender,
    That, like this sleek and seeing ball
    But a prick will make no eye at all,
    Where we, even where we mean
      To mend her we end her,
    When we hew or delve:
After-comers cannot guess the beauty been.
  Ten or twelve, only ten or twelve
    Strokes of havoc únselve
    The sweet especial scene,
    Rural scene, a rural scene,
    Sweet especial rural scene.

GERARD MANLEY HOPKINS (1844–1889)

190

When the leaves in autumn wither
    With a tawny tanned face,
Warped and wrinkled up together,
The year's late beauty to disgrace;
There thy life's glass may'st thou find thee:
    Green now, grey now, gone anon,
    Leaving, worldling, of thine own
Neither fruit nor leaf behind thee.

JOSHUA SYLVESTER

THE BURNING OF THE LEAVES

Now is the time for the burning of the leaves.
They go to the fire; the nostril pricks with smoke
Wandering slowly into a weeping mist.
Brittle and blotched, ragged and rotten sheaves!
A flame seizes the smouldering ruin and bites
On stubborn stalks that crackle as they resist.

The last hollyhock's falled tower is dust;
All the spices of June are a bitter reek,
All the extravagant riches spent and mean.
All burns! The reddest rose is a ghost;
Sparks whirl up, to expire in the mist: the wild
Fingers of fire are making corruption clean.

Now is the time for stripping the spirit bare,
Time for the burning of days ended and done,
Idle solace of things that have gone before:
Rootless hopes and fruitless desire are there;
Let them go to the fire, with never a look behind.
The world that was ours is a world that is ours no more.

They will come again, the leaf and the flower, to arise
From squalor of rottenness into the old splendour,
And magical scents to a wondering memory bring;
The same glory, to shine upon different eyes.
Earth cares for her own ruins, naught for ours.
Nothing is certain, only the certain spring.

LAURENCE BINYON (1869–1943)

NOVEMBER

Red o'er the forest peers the setting sun;
    The line of yellow light dies fast away
That crown'd the eastern copse; and chill and dun
    Falls on the moor the brief November day.

Now the tired hunter winds a parting note,
    And Echo bids good-night from every glade;
Yet wait awhile and see the calm leaves float
    Each to his rest beneath their parent shade.

How like decaying life they seem to glide
    And yet no second spring have they in store;
And where they fall, forgotten to abide
    Is all their portion, and they ask no more.

Soon o'er their heads blithe April airs shall sing,
    A thousand wild-flowers round them shall unfold,
The green buds glisten in the dews of Spring,
    And all be vernal rapture as of old.

Unconscious they in waste oblivion lie,
    In all the world of busy life around
No thought of them – in all the bounteous sky
    No drop, for them of kindly influence found.

Man's portion is to die and rise again:
    Yet he complains, while these unmurmuring part
With their sweet lives, as pure from sin and stain
    As his when Eden held his virgin heart.

JOHN KEBLE (1792–1866)

LORD, I AM LIKE TO MISTLETOE

Lord, I am like to mistletoe,
Which has no root and cannot grow
Or prosper, but by that same tree
It clings about: so I by thee.
What need I then to fear at all
So long as I about thee crawl?
But if that tree should fall and die,
Tumble shall heaven and so down will I.

ROBERT HERRICK (1591–1674)

194

Now the holly bears a berry as white as the milk,
And Mary bore Jesus, who was wrapped up in silk:

And Mary bore Jesus Christ our Saviour for to be,
And the first tree in the greenwood, it was the holly, holly, holly!
And the first tree in the greenwood, it was the holly.

Now the holly bears a berry as green as the grass,
And Mary bore Jesus, who died on the cross:

Now the holly bears a berry as black as the coal,
And Mary bore Jesus, who died for us all:

Now the holly bears a berry, as blood is it red,
Then trust we our Saviour, who rose from the dead:

ANONYMOUS

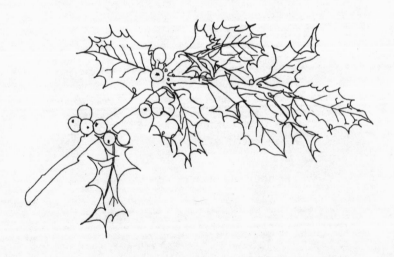

THE HOLLY AND THE IVY

The holly and the ivy,
When they are both full grown,
Of all the trees that are in the wood,
The holly bears the crown:
 The rising of the sun
 And the running of the deer,
 The playing of the merry organ,
 Sweet singing in the choir.

The holly bears a blossom,
As white as the lily flower,
And Mary bore sweet Jesus Christ,
To be our sweet Saviour:

The holly bears a berry,
As red as any blood,
And Mary bore sweet Jesus Christ
To do poor sinners good:

The holly bears a prickle,
As sharp as any thorn,
And Mary bore sweet Jesus Christ
On Christmas day in the morn:

The holly bears a bark,
As bitter as any gall,
And Mary bore sweet Jesus Christ
For to redeem us all:

The holly and the ivy,
When they are both full grown,
Of all the trees that are in the wood,
The holly bears the crown:

ANONYMOUS

O reader! hast thou ever stood to see
   The holly tree?
The eye, that contemplates it well, perceives
   Its glossy leaves,
Ordered by an intelligence so wise
As might confound the atheist's sophistries.

Below a circling fence, its leaves are seen
   Wrinkled and keen;
No grazing cattle, through their prickly round,
   Can reach to wound,
But as they grow where nothing is to fear,
Smooth and unarmed the pointless leaves appear.

I love to view these things with curious eyes,
   And moralize:
And in this wisdom of the holly tree
   Can emblems see
Wherewith, perchance, to make a pleasant rhyme,
One which may profit in the after-time.

Thus, though abroad, perchance, I might appear
   Harsh and austere;
To those, who on my leisure would intrude,
   Reserved and rude;
Gentle at home amid my friends I'd be
Like the high leaves upon the holly tree.

And should my youth, as youth is apt, I know,
   Some harshness show,
All vain asperities, I day by day
   Would wear away;
Till the smooth temper of my age should be
Like the high leaves upon the holly tree.

And as, when all the summer trees are seen
   So bright and green,
The holly leaves their fadeless lines display
   Less bright than they;
But when the bare and wintry woods we see,
What then so cheerful as the holly tree.

So serious should my youth appear among
   The thoughtless throng;
So would I seem, amid the young and gay,
   More grave than they;
That in my age as cheerful I might be
As the green winter of the holly tree.

ROBERT SOUTHEY (1774–1843)

198

Green groweth the holly,
So doth the ivy;
    Though winter blasts blow never so high,
Green groweth the holly.

Gay are the flowers,
Hedgerows and ploughlands;
    The days grow longer in the sun,
Soft fall the showers.

Full gold the harvest,
Grain for thy labour;
    With God must work for daily bread,
Else, man, thou starvest.

Fast fall the shed leaves,
Russet and yellow;
    But resting-beds are snug and safe
Where swung the dead leaves.

Green groweth the holly,
So doth the ivy;
    The God of life can never die,
Hope! saith the holly.

ANONYMOUS

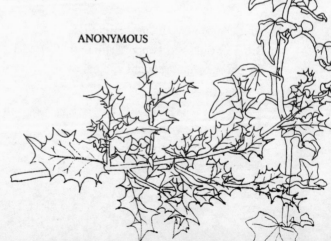

CHRISTMAS TREE

O bird of peace, bring me the Laurel,
Bring Bay, bring Olive to entwine
The sombre branches of my fir-tree,
To be a symbol and a sign:

Bring in your beak red English Roses,
Dew-fragrant still. From Italy
Bring Orange bloom, bee-haunted Lemon,
Both flower and fruit, to grace my tree.

From France bring Lilies of the valley
And set them so that every bell
Sways with the movement of the boughs
And swings into a silver peal.

And Edelweiss and skiey Gentian
Pluck from the snows: so Switzerland
Shall send her wise and mountain spirit
All strife and rage to countermand.

Sunflowers from Russia, and from Greece
Her wind-blown flower, Anemone,
From Norway Spruce, from Holland Tulips,
Our master fir from Germany.

And O, from Czech and Polish fields
Bring Cornflower, Poppy – and bring Corn
To gild the winter boughs and tell us
Death is dead and life new-born.

And O, my dove, when candle flames
Burn true and clear in midnight air,
Ascend my tree and plume your wings
And carol to the ancient star;

Yes, whistle, pipe and flute the carol,
Unto us is born a son
And, for a space, destroy division
And make the war-torn nations one.

VIOLA GARVIN

DOWN WITH THE ROSEMARY AND BAYS

Down with the rosemary and bays,
    Down with the mistletoe;
Instead of holly, now upraise
    The greener box, for show.

The holly hitherto did sway:
    Let box now domineer
Until the dancing Easter day,
    Or Easter's eve appear.

Then youthful box, which now hath grace
    Your houses to renew,
Grown old, surrender must his place
    Unto the crispèd yew.

When yew is out, then birch comes in,
    And many flowers beside,
Both of a fresh and fragrant kin,
    To honour Whitsuntide.

Green rushes then, and sweetest bents,
    With cooler oaken boughs,
Come in for comely ornaments,
    To readorn the house.

Thus times do shift; each thing his turn does hold;
New things succeed, as former things grow old.

ROBERT HERRICK (1591–1674)

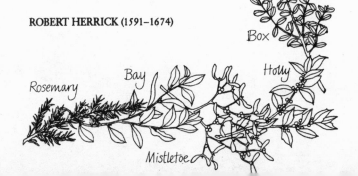

SPRING AND FALL
to a young child

Márgarét, áre you gríeving
Over Goldengrove unleaving?
Leáves líke the things of man, you
With your fresh thoughts care for, can you?
Ah! ás the heart grows older
It will come to such sights colder
By and by, nor spare a sigh
Though worlds of wanwood leafmeal lie;
And yet you will weep and know why.
Now no matter, child, the name:
Sórrow's spríngs áre the same.
Nor mouth had, no nor mind, expressed
What heart heard of, ghost guessed:
It ís the blight man was born for,
It is Margaret you mourn for.

GERARD MANLEY HOPKINS (1844–1889)

TO BLOSSOMS

Fair pledges of a fruitful tree,
Why do ye fall so fast?
Your date is not so past,
But you may stay yet here awhile
To blush and gently smile,
And go at last.

What! were ye born to be
An hour of half's delight,
And so to bid good night?
'Twas pity nature brought you forth
Merely to show your worth,
And lose you quite.

But ye are lovely leaves, where we
May read how soon things have
Their end, though ne'er so brave;
And after they have shown their pride,
Like you awhile, they glide
Into the grave.

ROBERT HERRICK (1591–1674)

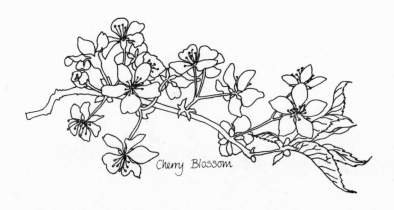

Cherry Blossom

Into the woods my master went,
Clean forspent, forspent;
Into the woods my master came,
Forspent with love and shame;
But the olives they were not blind to him,
The little grey leaves were kind to him,
The thorn tree had a mind to him,
When into the woods he came.

Out of the woods my master went,
And he was well content;
Out of the woods my master came,
Content with death and shame.
When death and shame would woo him last,
From under the trees they drew him last,
'Twas on a tree they slew him, last,
When out of the woods he came.

SIDNEY LANIER (1842–1881)

Our Church Palms Are Budding Willow Twigs

While Christ lay dead the widowed world
Wore willow green for hope undone:
Till, when bright Easter dews impearled
The chilly burial earth,
All north and south, all east and west,
Flushed rosy in the arising sun:
Hope laughed, and Faith resumed her rest,
And Love remembered mirth.

CHRISTINA ROSSETTI (1830–1894)

Lupin & Iris seedheads